GramMaR WoRKs!

15 Reproducible Skills Lessons that Teach Essential Grammar Rules

by Jim Halverson

SCHOLASTIC
PROFESSIONAL BOOKS

New York • Toronto • London • Auckland • Sydney

With thanks to my students and colleagues, past and present, at Saint Ann's School, and especially to Carol Rawlings, Ruth Chapman, Joanna Dean, Linda Kaufman, and Stanley Bosworth. With love to Anita and Leif.

Teachers may photocopy the designated reproducible pages for classroom use. No other part of this publication may be reproduced in whole or in part, or stored in a retrieval system, or transmitted in any form or by any means, electronic, mechanical, photocopying or otherwise, without written permission of the publisher. For information regarding permission, write to Scholastic, 555 Broadway, New York, 10012.

Cover illustration and design by Jaime Lucero
Interior design by Robert Dominguez and Jaime Lucero for Grafica, Inc.
Illustrations by Andy Myers

ISBN 0-590-60420-1

Copyright © 1996 by Jim Halverson. All rights reserved. Printed in the U.S.A.

Table of Contents

How to Use This Book

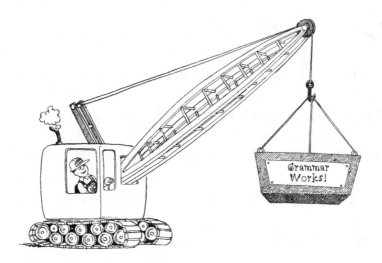

A New Approach

When I first began teaching, I found that many students equated learning punctuation and grammar with tedium and toil. Furthermore, even when students carefully and successfully completed traditional grammar exercises, the very problems that they seemed to have overcome on Monday turned up in their writing on Tuesday. I soon decided that my students needed a new approach to parts of speech, punctuation, and usage, one that made learning engaging, stimulating, meaningful, and fun.

I also wanted to break down the artificial barrier that so many students create between the content and the style of their writing, as if effective storytelling and argumentation have little to do with punctuation and usage. I realized that this kind of separation is the implicit message to students when mechanical skills are treated as ends in themselves rather than integral parts of the writing process. Too often we say, "That's enough grammar. Now it's time to write stories." To address this artificial separation, I wrote the exercises in this book as if they were themselves stories.

Finally, I created this approach in response to the diversity of student learning styles that I found in my classes. I needed materials to teach a whole class, to use in groups, or to hand out for individual study.

Grammar That Engages Students

Each unit is *interactive*. Instead of lessons that look like pages from a textbook, students will find **models** that lead them to discover the rules, **exercises** that are interesting stories, and **reviews** that are mazes.

Grammar Integrated Into Creative Writing

Every exercise is part of an appealing, ongoing story. In many cases students proofread a story they might have written themselves.

Reviews in Game Form

Each unit concludes with games, puzzles, and mazes that the students can do only if they have achieved an understanding of the concepts.

For Groups or Individuals

The concepts in each unit are illustrated with models that students can analyze in groups or on their own. Step-by-step instructions make it easy for students to understand the material.

How the Units Work

Students Discover

A short introductory section catches students' interest and alerts them to the focus of the unit. Models illustrate the correct patterns for standard written English. Through observation, analysis, and discussion, students work out the rules for themselves, a process that helps them internalize and retain the concepts more effectively than learning by rote. Students learn the rules by doing rather than by being told.

Students Confirm

The exercises in each unit make up a short, amusing story designed to capture students' interest as they practice what they have just learned. As the story moves toward its climax, the skills problems become more like the proofreading tasks every writer faces.

Students Review

Every unit ends with a review. The form of the review—secret codes, mazes—motivates students because it is fun. Again, the students are engaged, mastering the concepts in order to solve the puzzles.

Students Extend the Learning

The exercises not only tell stories but inspire classroom discussions. These can range from sharing funny anecdotes to debating difficult values questions. Above all, the stories stimulate students' own writing. What better way to reinforce the use of quotation marks than to have students write their own stories using punctuated dialogue?

Teacher-To-Teacher

First, read through the book.

You and your students will benefit the most from this book if you familiarize yourself with it first. Notice the range of topics, some more difficult, some less. Also note that some topics extend over two or three units. With an understanding of the units, you can then tailor the lessons to the needs of your class. To help introduce each unit, you will find a brief section of teaching notes that alerts you to specific teaching strategies and provides extensions of the material.

Decide on class use.

This book gives you the option of working on a single concept with the entire class or breaking the class into study groups, each with its own skills topic. Furthermore, if individuals need personalized lessons, they can work on a unit that fits their own remedial or enrichment requirements.

Keep the book's purpose in mind.

Keep alive the idea that grammar, punctuation, and usage are just tools of the writer's trade. As students begin to see themselves as writers, they will be motivated to master the use of these tools. An important benefit of this approach should soon emerge: you will be empowering students with the means to move through the proofreading and revision stages of the writing process.

Capitalization

This Unit Teaches Students

- when to capitalize
- how to distinguish between common and proper nouns and adjectives
- which nouns and adjectives are always capitalized

Getting Started

After looking at models of proper and common nouns and adjectives, students spot capitalization patterns and find the correct statements of the rules. Exercises provide immediate practice in identifying words that need to be capitalized. The exercise sentences develop the story about a place called Fantasy Street.

The concepts are reviewed at the end of the unit in a "secret code" puzzle and a maze that uses incorrectly capitalized words as blocks.

Teaching Notes

Students often have problems with capitalization, either through carelessness or because they have trouble grasping the concept of proper nouns and proper adjectives. Before handing out this unit, you may wish to go over the general rules of capitalization and play some preparatory oral "games" with the class. You might, for instance, have students tell how many capital letters there should be in these sentences:

- John went to the store and bought a candy bar. (1)
- John went to Cordero's Grocery and bought a pack of Hershey's Kisses. (5)
- John and I went to the store and bought a candy bar. (2)
- At the store John bought a pack of Trident. (3)

Students could then be asked to make up sentences for each other that include a certain number of capitalized words.

Capitalization

capital letters can be confusing for writers of english. because our language developed from many other languages, each with its own capitalization rules, the rules for capitalizing have often changed. many words that were capitalized in the past are no longer capitalized unless they begin a sentence, are the title of a poem, or are being used as a proper name. two examples are spring and fall.

What's It All About?

Did something seem 'wrong' or 'funny' to you when you read the paragraph at left? Of course—there was no capitalization! In fact, there are five capitalization errors in the paragraph. Circle the letters that should have been capitalized.

Let's Find Out

In each of the following model sentences, the same word has been used twice: once with a capital letter and once with a small letter. Your job is to figure out the rule that explains why the same word is capitalized in one place and not in another.

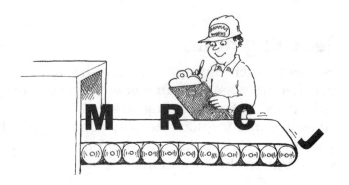

Model Sentences

1. "I think that spring is my favorite season," said a girl named Spring Summerall.

2. "Do you mean to say that of all the seasons, you like spring best?" asked Season Saxon, Spring's best friend.

3. Spring was born in spring. Can you guess what season it was when her sister Autumn was born?

Let's Try It

Two of these statements are correct. One is incorrect. Circle the two statements that are correct.

1. Capitalize the first word of a sentence.

2. Capitalize any word that names a person, place, or thing.

3. Capitalize any word that names a particular person, place, or thing.

DID YOU KNOW?

Capital letters are sometimes called uppercase letters. That's because in the past, when printers set rows of metal type by hand, they kept the letters in rows of wooden cases. The capital letters were in the upper cases, and the small letters were in the lower cases.

Let's Practice

Now that you're becoming a capitalization expert, test your skills by correcting the following sentences. Decide if the underlined words in each sentence are correct. Cross out and rewrite any incorrect words.

Example: My <u>street</u> is called <u>Fantasy</u> <s>street</s>. *Street*

1. <u>Fantasy Street</u> is really a very special <u>Street</u>.

2. <u>On</u> this <u>street</u> there is a <u>department Store</u> named <u>Rainbow's</u> that sells beautiful <u>dreams</u> and happy endings.

3. <u>there</u> is also a <u>hotel</u> called <u>The highrise hotel</u> that is forty stories <u>high</u> and is shaped like a <u>spacecraft</u>.

4. My <u>teacher</u>, <u>Mr. Gooden</u>, has a <u>home</u> on <u>fantasy Street</u>.

CAPITALIZING PROPER NOUNS AND ADJECTIVES

What's It All About?

Most nouns are called **common nouns** and are not capitalized. However, some words in English are always capitalized. These are **proper nouns** and **proper adjectives.** Other words such as *street* or *hotel* can be either proper nouns or common nouns depending on how you use them.

Nouns are words that name things. The word *boy* is a **common noun.** The word *Thomas* is a **proper noun.** Adjectives are words that describe things. In the following sentence two adjectives are underlined: "Matilda is a blonde Australian student." Can you tell which is the common adjective and which is the proper adjective?

Let's Find Out

The following sentences include many different proper nouns and adjectives. Read them carefully. Use them to help you do the activity on page 11.

Model Sentences

1. On Fantasy Street there is a school that gives the usual courses in mathematics, history, English, and Spanish.

2. It also offers courses on unusual subjects like grapefruit trees, kangaroos, Mars, and French poodles.

3. Many of the people who live on Fantasy Street are from Spanish, Italian, and African backgrounds.

4. They practice different religions such as Christianity, Judaism, and Islam and celebrate holidays such as Chinese New Year, Christmas, and Ramadan.

5. The children fly exotic kites in the spring and play ball games when school lets out in June.

6. On Saturdays dog walkers stop to chat as their French poodles and German shepherds sniff for birds and rabbits.

7. Friends zoom by on skates and on their favorite brand of skateboard, the Rocket Racer.

Let's Try It

Make a check next to each group below that names proper nouns and adjectives that are *always* capitalized. Rewrite any underlined words that need capitalization. Use the model sentences on page 10–11 to help you.

1. names of languages like french

2. names of religions like Islam

3. names of school subjects that are not languages or religions, such as math

4. days of the week like wednesday

5. names of the months like february

6. names of holidays like Memorial Day

7. names of animals like lion

8. names of seasons like spring

9. names of brands like ford

10. names of countries and nationalities like ireland and irish

11. parts of names that mention countries or nationalities like french bread

12. names of planets like saturn

DID YOU KNOW?

In English the word proper usually means "fitting" or "appropriate." It comes from the Latin word proprius, which means "one's own." The terms proper noun and proper adjective are closer in meaning to the Latin definition.

Let's Practice

Decide if the underlined words in each sentence are correct. Cross out and rewrite any incorrect words.

Example: The <u>students</u> were studying ~~sp<s>a</s>sh~~ *Spanish* and ~~H<s>i</s>story~~ *history*.

1. Every <u>wednesday</u> at Fantasy School the <u>students</u> study <u>math</u>, <u>spanish</u>, and the habits of <u>kangaroos</u>.

2. School lets out for special <u>holidays</u> like <u>easter</u> in the <u>Spring</u> and <u>Thanksgiving</u> in the <u>fall</u>, but it also closes for unusual <u>holidays</u> in <u>may</u> like <u>wildflower</u> <u>day</u> when everyone goes into the <u>woods</u> to admire <u>wildflowers</u>.

3. When <u>Students</u> of <u>mexican</u> background celebrate the <u>Mexican</u> national <u>holiday</u> on <u>may</u> 5, everyone in the class joins them in eating a spicy brand of <u>tortilla</u> <u>chips</u> called <u>Caliente</u> <u>chips</u>.

4. In addition to a peculiar <u>professor</u> named <u>professor</u> <u>Whatnot</u>, the <u>teachers</u> at Fantasy School have interesting backgrounds and include <u>Russian</u> <u>artists</u>, <u>japanese</u> <u>cooks</u>, and an <u>alaskan</u> <u>elk</u> <u>herder</u>.

FUN WITH CAPITALIZATION

Capitalization Code

Here's a secret code. If you look carefully, you'll see that many words have been run together. Some of the words are proper nouns that always need capitalization. Circle the first letter of each proper noun. Then write those words correctly. The capital letters will help you find a hidden message.

Example:

happyhawaiidogcatenglandflowerlondonteacherlarryandoslo

Hawaii   **E**ngland   **L**ondon   **L**arry   **O**slo

The hidden word is HELLO.

Your coded lines:

floorskygeorgiaappleohiopigoklahomasillyropestroubledavid

waterjuneunderflameopenoregonshirtmilebookbatboliviapencil

Capitalization Maze

Ready to test your knowledge of proper nouns and adjectives? The maze has 29 words. Some of them are capitalized correctly; some are not. As you come to each word, decide if it is correct or not. If the word is correct, you may pass through it. If a word is incorrect, it is like a wall and you cannot go through it. The path to the finish goes through 15 correctly written words.

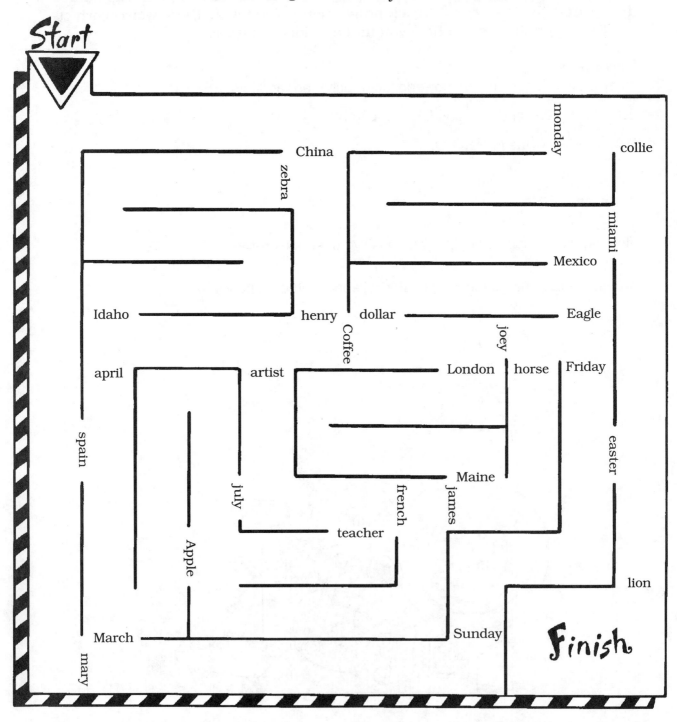

Capitalization Student Page

Punctuation of Items in a Series

This Unit Teaches Students

- when to use commas to separate items in a series

Getting Started

Students study model sentences that illustrate the use of commas in series of three or more. They use these models to discover the rule and then apply what they have learned in exercises. The exercise sentences tell a story about a family at breakfast.

To review the material, there are two punctuation "games" at the end of the unit—a "secret code" and a maze where incorrect punctuation acts as blocks.

Teaching Notes

Before handing the material out, you may wish to review the meaning of *series* (a list or a set of like grammatical terms) as it is used in this lesson. Write the following sentence on the chalkboard:

Jane Harvey Pepe Tyler and Bunny are absent today.

Ask: How many people are mentioned. Is it three people—Jane Harvey and Pepe Tyler and Bunny? Is it five people—Jane, Harvey, Pepe, Tyler, and Bunny? Discuss how commas help to make the meaning clear.

Some stylists prefer to omit the comma before *and* in a series—peas, corn and carrots—but this unit sides with the majority and uses that comma—peas, corn, and carrots. You may wish to let students know that this comma is optional.

Punctuation of Items in a Series

What's It All About?

When you group several names or make a list, you are writing a series of things. To make your meaning clear, you must often separate these items with commas.

Let's Find Out

In the sentences below the *items in a series* are printed in italics. In some sentences the items are separated with commas, while in others there are no commas. See if you can discover the key to this difference.

Teresa went to the game with Mary Lou George and Sue.

How many people went to the game with Teresa?

Did she go with four people—Mary, Lou, George, and Sue? Did she go with three—Mary Lou, George, and Sue? or with only two—a girl named Mary Lou George and a girl named Sue?

Can you see how commas would have helped this writer be clear?

Model Sentences

1. Mayor Sandra Santos of New Town has three children named *Keisha, Kendra, and Hal.*

2. The family also has *four computers and two dogs.*

3. Sandra Santos's husband Nelson *works, plays, and shops* on these computers.

4. The family's two dogs are called *Chewie and Pal.*

5. Pal got his name because he is a *very friendly, affectionate, and loyal* dog.

6. Chewie was given his name because he *gnaws on bones, chomps on slippers, and chews on shoes.*

7. *Mayor Santos, her husband, her children, and their dogs* make up a *very amusing and interesting* family.

Look at sentences 1 and 2. In the first sentence commas have been used to separate the items. In the second sentence there are no commas. Similarly, in sentence 3 there are commas, but not in 4. Do you see the reason?

Hint: The answer lies in the number of items in each series.

Let's Try It

Use the model sentences to complete these exercises:

1. In sentence 7 there are two different sets of items in a series.

a) Underline each of them.

b) How many items are in the first set? _____

c) How many items are in the second set? _____

2. Underline the sentence below that best expresses the rule for using commas to separate items in a series.

a) Separate the items in a series with commas when there are **three** or more.

b) Separate the items in a series with commas when there are **two** or more.

c) To flavor your sentences, sprinkle them lightly with commas to fit your taste.

3. In sentence 6 entire groups of words are followed by commas. Underline the sentence below that best expresses the reason for this.

a) Each group of words is a phrase, and phrases can make up items in a series.

b) You put a comma after every noun (naming word) in a sentence.

c) It looks better that way.

Let's Practice

Read the sentences. Decide if the commas are used correctly or not. In some sentences you must add commas in the boxes provided. In others you must cross out incorrect commas. You may wish to look back at the model sentences for help.

Example: Kendra[,] Keisha[,] and Hal are Mayor Santos's three[✗] young children.

1. Kendra[ ] Keisha[ ] and Hal had just fed Pal[,] and Chewie and were ready for their own breakfast.

2. Their mother asked, "Keisha[ ] Kendra[ ] and Hal, would you like orange juice[ ] or tea?"

3. Keisha[,] and Hal asked for orange juice, and Kendra, who always loved to be different, asked for a mixture of orange juice[,] milk[,] and tea.

4. "Forgive me for saying so, but that is silly[ ] disgusting[,] and wasteful," said their father, who was always honest[,] and outspoken.

5. "That's very true," said Kendra. "But I'm doing a food[ ] and drink experiment to discover which breakfast drinks are delicious[ ] nutritious[ ] colorful[,] and fun."

6. Kendra took a sip of the mixture[ ] made a face like a Halloween pumpkin's[ ] and spat it back into the glass, saying, "That's not so delicious[ ] nutritious[ ] colorful[ ] or fun!"

Punctuation of Items in a Series
Student Page

Challenge

These bonus sentences have no boxes to help you. Add any commas that are needed.

1. Keisha and Hal were winking smiling and laughing.

2. They watched as Kendra took a bowl of cereal poured milk on it and added some honey but no tea or orange juice.

3. After Kendra Keisha and Hal had finished their breakfast, they thanked their mother and father for a very healthful enjoyable and amusing meal.

FUN WITH COMMAS

Secret Message

Find the secret message in the sentences below. Add commas wherever they are missing. Then underline the first letter of the word *after* each comma that you added. The underlined letters make up a word for each sentence.

Example: The New Town Zoo features tigers, hyenas, buffalo, elephants, wolves, lions, leopards, otters, and monkeys. **Message:** Hello.

1. My favorite colors are blue yellow orange, and red, and my favorite objects are sailboats, clocks umbrellas, and balloons.

2. The airline flies to Holland, Mexico Canada Austria, Brazil, France Norway, and Japan.

3. The teacher read us a surprising unusual strange, vivid exciting, and thoroughly enchanting story.

4. At the grocery we bought potatoes, onions cabbage, butter oranges meat, cookies milk apples sugar, and bread.

Punctuation Maze

Complete the maze by following the correctly punctuated sentences. If a box contains incorrect punctuation, it is like a wall of the maze. You cannot go through it. The correct path to the finish will take you through 10 boxes.

Start

My cat is cute, sweet, and smart.

His shirt has red blue and gray stripes.

My dog is big, and brawny.

It's windy, and cold outside.

I'd like salad rice, and milk.

Bring your books, paper, and pens.

The worker was sweating, panting, and groaning.

How, when, and why did you come?

This path seems too easy too obvious, and too short.

I am both wary, and suspicious of shortcuts.

Meg, Mandy, and Min met my Mom.

The teacher was both sweet, and strict.

Your work was thoughtful, wise, and successful.

At meals I never whistle, or yodel.

Patience, work, and skill will be rewarded.

Finish

This maze has been long, hard, and challenging.

This path is also blocked, and misleading.

The movie was short, exciting, and scary.

I hope I wish, and I beg for this to be right.

You can't jump, climb, or slip to the finish.

Basic Punctuation: Dates, Cities, States, and Countries

This Unit Teaches Students

- how to use commas when writing dates
- how to use commas to set off cities, states, and countries

Getting Started

The unit is divided into two sections. The first part focuses on using commas in dates. The exercises deal with a fictional town called Timetrip where the inhabitants live in past time. The second part of the unit focuses on commas used to separate cities, states, and countries.

The unit concludes with a punctuation maze.

Teaching Notes

The two parts of the unit reinforce the same punctuation concept—that the second element in a date or in a city/state or city/country combination is *set off* with commas. Begin by introducing the concept of *set off*. On the chalkboard write sentences such as:

- **November 28, 1996, was Thanksgiving Day.**
- **Santiago, Chile, is Maria's hometown.**

Discuss how *1996* and *Chile* are separated from the rest of the sentence because they are set off with commas.

Basic Punctuation: Dates, Cities, States, and Countries

What's It All About?

As you can see in the box at right, there are many different ways to write a date. A formal wedding invitation usually spells out every word and numeral. A quick note might abbreviate the month or just use numerals. In Europe people often write the day before the month—31/10/97 instead of 10/31/97. When you write, you should follow the usual pattern for dates used in the United States.

> The thirty-first day of October, Nineteen Hundred Ninety-Seven
> October 31, 1997
> Oct. 31, 1997
> 10/31/97
> 31 October 1997

USING COMMAS WITH DATES

Let's Find Out

Notice the dates in the sentences below. See if you can discover the correct pattern.

Model Sentences

1. The town of Timetrip was founded on June 1, 1950.

2. Timetrip seems more like a town from June 1, 1900, than a modern town.

3. Although Mavis Max, the mayor of Timetrip, was born on September 23, 1960, she wears a silk bonnet from 1870.

When a date includes the month, day, and year (October 26, 1937), the year is *set off with commas*. Usually *set off* means that *two* commas are used, one before and one after the year as in model sentences 2 and 3. Sometimes only one comma is needed—when the year comes at the very end of the sentence (model 1).

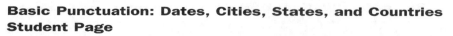

Let's Try It

Underline the sentence in which the date is correctly punctuated. You may look back at the model sentences if you need to.

1. (a) Morris Miter was born on September 23 1960.

   (b) Morris Miter was born on September, 23, 1960.

   (c) Morris Miter was born on September 23, 1960.

2. (a) June 1, 1950, was the day that Timetrip was founded.

   (b) June, 1 1950, was the day that Timetrip was founded.

   (c) June 1, 1950 was the day that Timetrip was founded.

3. (a) Mayor Max's dress is more typical of, 1890, than 1990.

   (b) Mayor Max's dress is more typical of 1890, than 1990.

   (c) Mayor Max's dress is more typical of 1890 than 1990.

Let's Practice

In the sentences below some of the dates are incorrectly punctuated. Your challenge is to correct the ones that are wrong. Add commas in the boxes if they are needed. Cross out incorrect punctuation. If necessary, you may look back at the model sentences.

Example: June ☒ 1 ☐, 1950 ☐, was the day that Timetrip was founded.

1. On September 10 ☐ 1996 ☐, Mayor Max's children rode to school in a horse-drawn carriage that was made on August ☐ 15 ☐ 1888 ☐ with hand tools.

2. Like most schools that year, their school opened on September 8 ☐ 1996 ☐ and closed for the summer on June ☐, 14 ☐, 1997.

3. Ten-year-old Marina Max practices penmanship with a fountain pen dated November 22 ☐ 1924 ☐ and reads from a primer first published on January ☐ 29 ☐, 1887 ☐ in England.

4. Marina's brother Todd, who was born on April ☐, 15 ☐ 1986 ☐ and is older than Marina, plays baseball with a handmade ash bat dated August ☐ 6 ☐ 1934.

COMMAS

USING COMMAS WITH CITIES, STATES, AND COUNTRIES

What's It All About?

As you can see from the box at right, the punctuation between cities, states, and countries follows much the same pattern as the punctuation of dates.

> February 29, 1900
> Kokomo, Indiana
> Your Town, U.S.A.
> Tokyo, Japan

Model Sentences

1. Timetrip is nothing like Boston, Massachusetts, or San Francisco, California.

2. It seems like London, England, during the last century.

Let's Try It

Circle the letter of the sentence that is correctly punctuated. Use the model sentences to help you.

1. (a) Boston Massachusetts seems more modern than Timetrip.

   (b) Boston, Massachusetts, seems more modern than Timetrip.

   (c) Boston, Massachusetts seems more modern than Timetrip.

2. (a) Mayor Max dresses like a woman from London, England in 1890.

   (b) Mayor Max dresses like a woman from London England in 1890.

   (c) Mayor Max dresses like a woman from London, England, in 1890.

Let's Practice

Read each sentence below. Decide if you should add commas or cross out incorrect punctuation. If necessary, you may look back at the model sentences.

Example: Boston▯ Massachusetts▯ seems more modern than⤫ Timetrip.

1. Mayor Mavis Max would prefer an old city like New Orleans▯ Louisiana▯ to a modern one like Las Vegas▯ Nevada.

2. She would like the cable cars of San Francisco▯ California▯ better than the high speed trains of Tokyo▯ Japan▯ that go over a hundred miles an hour.

3. Given a choice between the rocket launchings of Cape Canaveral▯ Florida▯ and the horse farms of Lexington▯ Kentucky▯ she would choose the horse farms for a visit.

4. Do you think she would prefer to go to Rome▯ or Miami▯ for a vacation?

Putting It All Together

Correct the mistakes in the sentences below. Add commas where needed, and cross out incorrectly placed commas.

1. Mayor Max of Timetrip seems so old-fashioned that you would think she was born on September▯ 23▯ 1860▯ instead of September▯ 23▯ 1960.

2. The mayor's neighbor, Paul Pierce, who was born in Geewhiz▯ Georgia▯ on July▯ 14▯ 1970▯ is even more old-fashioned than the mayor.

3. He wears formal suits that could have been seen in Paris▯ France▯ on July▯ 14▯ 1770.

4. Why don't they choose to live in a modern place like Las Vegas▯ Nevada▯ instead of Timetrip, which seems like New Orleans▯ Louisiana▯ 150 years ago?

Challenge

These sentences have no boxes. Add commas where they are needed.

1. As Paul Pierce says, "Our country was born on July 4 1776 when the world seemed less complicated than on July 4 1976."

2. Mayor Max agrees, "If we can't live somewhere exciting like San Francisco California, then we can at least try to make Timetrip into a place like Philadelphia Pennsylvania during the Revolutionary War.

3. Do you agree that Timetrip would be more fun today than Chicago Illinois or Paris France?

4. Would you rather be born on September 19 1990, in Dallas Texas than on September 19, 1890 in London England?

Punctuation Maze

Complete the maze by following the correctly punctuated sentences. If a box contains incorrect punctuation, it is like a wall of the maze. You cannot go through it. The correct path to the finish will take you through nine boxes.

Start

May 1, 1992, was very hot.

I live in Boise Idaho.

On June 3 1993 it rained on me.

It rarely rains in Cairo, Egypt, in May.

In 1996 I'm moving to Cleveland Ohio.

Oslo Norway is far north.

She lives in Toledo, Ohio.

My cat was born on May 10, 1994.

I graduated on June 30 1995.

July 4, 1976 was special.

In Taos, New Mexico is Kit Carson's home.

I love Ogden Utah.

It is winter in July in Santiago Chile.

In Rome, Italy, we ate pasta.

We visited Williamsburg, Virginia.

On October 26, 1987, I was born.

Portland Maine, has a beautiful harbor.

February 29, 1992, was a Leap Day.

He left Alta Utah in 1980.

December 21, 1845, was a very cold day.

She works in Chicago Illinois.

Finish

**Basic Punctuation: Dates, Cities, States, and Countries
Student Page**

Using Quotation Marks

This Unit Teaches Students
- how to distinguish between direct and indirect quotations
- how to punctuate quotations at the end of sentences
- how to punctuate quotations at the beginning of sentences

Getting Started

Students study models that illustrate direct and indirect quotations and then complete exercises in which they distinguish the two forms. Next, students focus on direct quotations that end a sentence or begin a sentence. In the final challenging exercises, students find and correct errors themselves, much as they do when proofreading their own stories.

The exercises tell about a brother and sister who decide to play detective to find out if their mother is giving their father a surprise party.

The unit concludes with a maze that uses sentences with errors to block the incorrect paths.

Teaching Notes

Begin by introducing the concept of direct vs. indirect quotations. Write these sentences on the board, and ask why one sentence needs quotation marks but the other doesn't.

- My mother said that I have to go the dentist.
- My mother said, "You have to go to the dentist."

Help students understand that direct quotes are the exact words that someone said and are always set off with quotation marks.

Write the same quotation twice on the board, once as the beginning of a sentence and once as the end:

- He said, "You look happy today."
- "You look happy today," he said.

See if students can understand the logic of the extra capitalization in the first sentence—i.e., that *He* begins the narrator's sentence and *You* begins the speaker's sentence. Point out that there is no need for an extra capital in the second sentence because *You* serves as the first word of both the speaker's sentence and the narrator's sentence.

Using Quotation Marks

Different kinds of writers punctuate speech in different ways. For example, a novelist might write:

Sandra Mason said, "We need a detective to get to the bottom of this mystery!"

A playwright's style:

Cary (enthusiastically) : Brilliant! Let's get started.

What's It All About?

As good writers know, human beings are constantly talking. People love to hear what others have to say and to tell their own tales. Books and stories are usually full of conversations. News articles include interesting and informative quotations, and plays consist almost entirely of dialogue. In this unit you will learn to punctuate quotations correctly in your own writing.

Let's Find Out

Before you learn <u>how</u> to use quotation marks, you must first know <u>when</u> to use them. In indirect quotations they are not needed at all. The sentences that follow have two kinds of quotations—direct and indirect. See if you can discover the difference.

Model Sentences

1. Sandra Mason told her brother Cary that she was sure that their mother was planning a surprise party. **(Indirect quotation)**

2. Cary said, "It is Dad's birthday on Saturday." **(Direct quotation)**

3. "Have you heard her whispering on the phone?" asked Sandra. **(Direct quotation)**

4. Cary nodded and said that their mother hung up suddenly when he and Dad walked into the room. **(Indirect quotation)**

Let's Try It

The model sentences illustrate the differences between direct and indirect quotations. In a **direct quotation** the speaker's exact words are enclosed in quotation marks and are set off from the rest of the sentence with a comma. An **indirect quotation** does not give the speaker's precise words and usually is not set off with commas. Notice also that an indirect quotation is often preceded by the word *that*.

After each of these sentences, put a **D** for direct quotation or an **I** for indirect quotation.

a) Sandra Mason said eagerly, "I think the party will be on Saturday."　　( )

b) Cary said that they didn't know for sure about the surprise party.　　( )

c) Sandra agreed that they needed more evidence.　　( )

d) "Let's play detectives and find out for sure," said Cary.　　( )

PUNCTUATION OF DIRECT QUOTATIONS

As you have seen, indirect quotations need no extra punctuation. Direct quotations, however, need punctuation and capitalization. Observe the following sentences. Be sure to notice what happens when the quotation comes first in the sentence and when it comes last.

Model Sentences

Quotation Ending the Sentence:

1. Sandra said, "So far we've only seen Mom acting suspiciously." **(Statement)**

2. Cary asked, "Where can we find more evidence?" **(Question)**

3. Sandra exclaimed, "We'll search for clues!" **(Exclamation)**

Quotation Starting the Sentence:

4. "Let's search her bedroom!" cried Cary. **(Exclamation)**

5. "But what will we say if she sees us?" asked Sandra. **(Question)**

6. "We'll just tell her we know what's happening. We'll say we just wanted to be part of the surprise," said Cary. **(Statement)**

Let's Try It

Use the model sentences to help you answer the following questions. Circle the right answers.

1. Where do you put the commas, periods, question marks, and exclamation points after a direct quotation?

   (a) Inside the quotation marks.

   (b) Outside the quotation marks.

2. When do you have to use an extra capital letter in direct quotations?

   (a) When the quotation begins the sentence.

   (b) When the quotation ends the sentence.

In the next five exercises, circle the letters of the correctly punctuated sentences:

3. a) Sandra said, "look, Cary, here's wrapping paper in Mom's closet."

   b) Sandra said "Look, Cary, here's wrapping paper in Mom's closet."

   c) Sandra said, "Look, Cary, here's wrapping paper in Mom's closet."

4. a) Cary asked, "What's underneath that stack of sweaters?"

   b) Cary asked, "what's underneath that stack of sweaters?"

   c) Cary asked? "What's underneath that stack of sweaters."

5. a) "She has one, two, three, four boxes hidden there," exclaimed Sandra!

   b) "She has one, two, three, four boxes hidden there!" Exclaimed Sandra.

   c) "She has one, two, three, four boxes hidden there!" exclaimed Sandra.

6. a) "Shall I try to open them?" asked Cary.

   b) "Shall I try to open them," asked Cary?

   c) Shall I try to open them? Asked Cary.

7. a) "No, you can't! They're sealed with tape" said Sandra!

   b) "No, you can't! They're sealed with tape," said Sandra.

   c) "No, you can't! They're sealed with tape" Said Sandra.

Let's Practice

Read the sentences and decide if the punctuation and capitalization in the boxes is correct. Your job is to find the errors and correct them. Add any needed punctuation. Put an X over any boxes containing mistakes, and write the correction above it.

Example: "Those boxes in Mom's closet were surely presents☐" X aid Sandra☐.

1. Cary said to his sister☐"I☐t seems absolutely sure now that

    Mom's giving Dad a surprise party☐"

2. Sandra suddenly frowned and asked? "i☐sn't Dad supposed to take us

    to the dentist on Saturday afternoon?"

3. "Yes, he is. That means the party can't be that afternoon☐" S☐aid Cary☐.

4. "Can we figure out when it is going to start☐" a☐sked Sandra?

5. Cary pondered and then proudly said☐ "w☐e surely can☐ "

6. "What have you thought of?" A☐sked Sandra?

7. "Mom's going to have all Dad's friends come while we're at the dentist,

    and when we drive in—SURPRISE☐" e☐xclaimed Cary!

**Using Quotation Marks
Student Page**

Challenge

Find the mistakes in these sentences. Add the necessary punctuation marks. Cross out incorrect lowercase letters and write capitals above them. Be careful: One of these sentences is an indirect quotation.

1. Sandra and Cary's father asked were you planning to do anything today now that you've had your teeth cleaned

2. No, Dad, I think we should go straight home said Sandra

3. Cary said that he wanted to go straight home too

4. There aren't any extra cars here exclaimed Cary when they drove into their driveway

5. Were you expecting someone to come over today asked his father

6. As the children walked into the house, their mother called out surprise

7. These new fishing rods and tackle boxes are for you and Cary because you did so well in school this year said their father

8. Their mother smiled and added we waited until your dentist appointments were over and you were free to go fishing with us

9. Thanks, Mom! You don't know just how much you surprised us said Sandra with a wink at Cary

Quotations Maze

Complete the maze by following the correctly written quotations. If you come to an oval that contains incorrect punctuation or capitalization, stop and go back. You cannot get through that path. The correct path to the finish will take you through seven ovals containing correct quotations. Caution: Some ovals that are correct lead to false paths. **Bonus:** How many correct ovals are there in the entire maze?

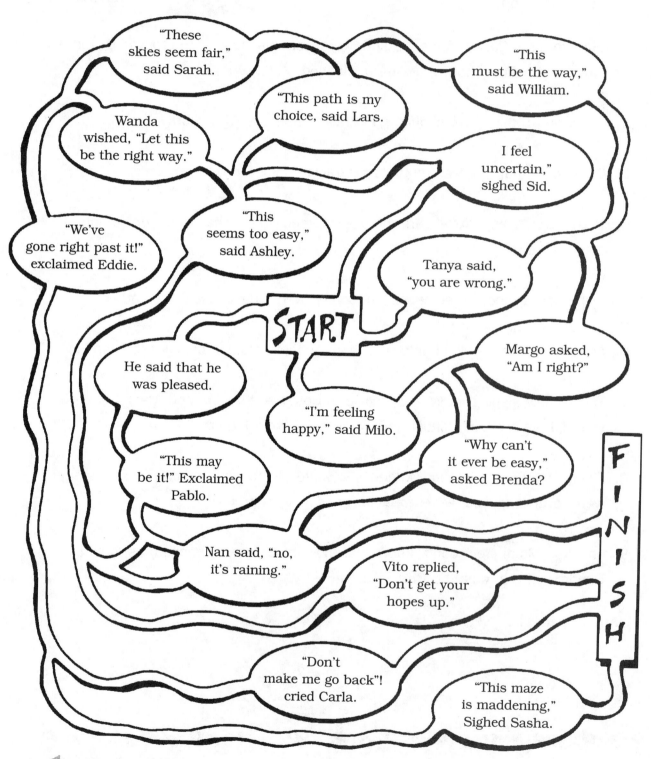

"These skies seem fair," said Sarah.

"This must be the way," said William.

"This path is my choice, said Lars.

Wanda wished, "Let this be the right way."

I feel uncertain," sighed Sid.

"We've gone right past it!" exclaimed Eddie.

"This seems too easy," said Ashley.

Tanya said, "you are wrong."

START

He said that he was pleased.

Margo asked, "Am I right?"

"I'm feeling happy," said Milo.

"Why can't it ever be easy," asked Brenda?

"This may be it!" Exclaimed Pablo.

Nan said, "no, it's raining."

Vito replied, "Don't get your hopes up."

FINISH

"Don't make me go back"! cried Carla.

"This maze is maddening," Sighed Sasha.

**Using Quotation Marks
Student Page**

More on Using Quotation Marks

This Unit Teaches Students

- about direct and indirect quotations
- about simple direct quotations
- about quotations interrupted by explanatory material

Getting Started

This unit reviews the material in the last unit and then adds new information about using quotations that are interrupted by the narrator's explanatory material. After students see models that illustrate indirect and direct quotations, they move on to models of interrupted quotations. These require not just knowledge of punctuating quotations, but an understanding of sentence fragments and run-ons as well. "True and False" questions require students to analyze the models carefully, discover the rules for themselves, and then apply the rules in the exercises.

The exercise sentences in this unit tell about a rebellion by disgruntled kitchen appliances.

The unit concludes with a maze that uses sentences with errors as blocks to the incorrect paths.

Teaching Notes

Some students may need to review sentence structure before starting this unit. If your students do not yet have a good grasp of both sentence fragments and run-on sentences (note the later units in this book), they may have difficulty with interrupted quotations. You may wish to use the prior unit on quotations early in the year and withhold this unit until later for review and enrichment—after you have done the fragment and run-on units.

Although this unit may prove challenging for some students, it can also be an incentive for others to take their style, not to mention their punctuation, to a new level of sophistication.

More on Using Quotation Marks

What's It All About?

In the box at right you see four different ways of presenting the same quotation. While the idea of what Warren says never changes, each of the sentences has a different rhythm. Good writers don't just give their characters interesting things to say. They also vary the way that they make their characters speak. To be a good writer you need to know how to punctuate quotations in each of these ways. You can learn how in this unit.

1. Warren said that he could wiggle his nose but not his ears.

2. Warren said, "I can wiggle my nose but not my ears."

3. "I can wiggle my nose but not my ears," Warren said.

4. "I can wiggle my nose," Warren said, "but not my ears."

REVIEW OF DIRECT AND INDIRECT QUOTATIONS

Model Sentences

1. "Those humans are mistreating me again," moaned Toby Toaster.

2. Rodney Refrigerator asked, "Toby Toaster, are you whining again?"

3. "You just try being a toaster for a day!" exclaimed Toby.

4. Rodney replied, "It would be quite nice to be warm inside for a change."

5. Toby said that he'd gladly trade a cold tummy for the heartburn the humans gave him every morning.

6. "Toby, you make me laugh," scoffed Steve Stove. "When they fire my oven up, the heat lasts hours, not just minutes."

These sentences illustrate the ways that quotations can be written. In this unit we will review three ways of punctuating quotations (model sentences 1-5) and introduce a fourth method (model sentence 6).

Let's Try It

Using the model sentences on page 38 for clues, find the answers to the following questions. Circle the correct answers.

1. Which sentence is an indirect quotation that needs no extra commas or quotation marks?

    Number: 1   2   3   4   5   6

2. When a quotation is a question or exclamation, where do you put the question mark or exclamation point?

    (a) Always at the end of the sentence.

    (b) After the quotation and inside the quotation marks.

    (c) After the quotation and outside the quotation marks.

3. If the quotation is a statement and ends the sentence, what two extra changes must you make?

    (a) You must set it off with a comma and capitalize the first word of the quotation.

    (b) You must set it off with an extra period and capitalize the first word of the quotation.

    (c) You must set it off with a comma and put an extra period at the end of the sentence.

4. If the quotation comes at the beginning of the sentence, do you need an extra capital letter after the quotation?

    (a) Yes

    (b) No

DID YOU KNOW?

If writers began every quotation the same way, stories would get repetitious and annoying. For example:

Mary said, "Hi."
Keena said, "How are you."
Then Mary said, "Fine."
Then Keena said, "I'm glad."

Let's Practice

In the following exercises, circle the letters of the correctly punctuated sentences:

1. (a) "What can I do?" Asked Toby Toaster.

   (b) "What can I do," asked Toby Toaster?

   (c) "What can I do?" asked Toby Toaster.

2. (a) Rodney Refrigerator laughed, "you often burn their toast."

   (b) Rodney Refrigerator laughed, "You often burn their toast."

   (c) Rodney Refrigerator laughed "you often burn their toast."

3. (a) Toby exclaimed, "That burns me too!"

   (b) Toby exclaimed, "that burns me too!"

   (c) Toby exclaimed! "That burns me too."

4. (a) "Toby, can't you be like me and just accept your fate", asked Steve Stove?

   (b) "Toby, can't you be like me and just accept your fate?" asked Steve Stove.

   (c) "Toby, can't you be like me and just accept your fate," asked Steve Stove?

5. (a) "Maybe he doesn't have to," said Rodney Refrigerator.

   (b) "Maybe he doesn't have to," Said Rodney Refrigerator.

   (c) "Maybe he doesn't have to" said Rodney Refrigerator.

6. (a) Toby replied, "that he didn't see what he could do to improve his life."

   (b) Toby replied that he didn't see what he could do to improve his life.

   (c) Toby replied, "That he didn't see what he could do to improve his life."

7. (a) Rodney asked, "have you ever really tried to foil the humans?"

   (b) Rodney asked, "Have you ever really tried to foil the humans"?

   (c) Rodney asked, "Have you ever really tried to foil the humans?"

8. (a) "No, that never occurred to me. They seem to have control over everything I do," Answered Toby Toaster.

   (b) "No, that never occurred to me. They seem to have control over everything I do." answered Toby Toaster.

   (c) "No, that never occurred to me. They seem to have control over everything I do," answered Toby Toaster.

INTERRUPTED QUOTATIONS

In Number 8 of the last exercise Toby spoke two sentences. That quotation could have been written in other ways, with the words *answered Toby Toaster* interrupting what he said, as you can see in the next set of model sentences.

Model Sentences

1. "No, that never occurred to me," answered Toby Toaster. "They seem to have control over everything I do."

2. "No," answered Toby Toaster, "that never occurred to me. They seem to have control over everything I do."

This method of writing quotations is used by writers to change the rhythm of their dialogue. If you are very observant, you will see that these last two model sentences vary somewhat in their punctuation and capitalization.

Let's Try It

Write **T** for **True** or **F** for **False** after each statement about the last two model sentences.

1. The punctuation immediately <u>after</u> the words *answered Toby Toaster* is the same in each sentence. ( )

2. Sentence 1 has a period after *answered Toby Toaster* while sentence 2 has a comma. ( )

3. The second part of the quotation—the part after *answered Toby Toaster*—begins with a capital letter in both sentences. ( )

4. There is a period after *answered Toby Toaster* in sentence 1 because both of his quotations are complete thoughts. ( )

5. There is a comma instead of a period after *answered Toby Toaster* in sentence 2 because Toby has not finished speaking yet. ( )

6. There is a comma instead of a period after *answered Toby Toaster* in sentence 2 because the first part of the quotation is not yet a complete thought. ( )

7. The quotation after the words *answered Toby Toaster* begins with a capital letter in sentence 2. ( )

8. The quotation after the words *answered Toby Toaster* begins with a capital letter in sentence 1 because that is the beginning of a new complete thought. ( )

The true-and-false questions above should have helped you see that you must look very carefully to decide if you are interrupting a complete thought when you write quotations this way. Now see if you can find the correctly punctuated sentences on the next page.

Let's Practice

Circle the letters of the correct sentences.

1. (a) "I don't think," said Steve Stove, "that Toby Toaster should try anything foolish."

   (b) "I don't think," said Steve Stove. "That Toby Toaster should try anything foolish."

2. (a) "Why not try to make the humans stop using him?" asked Rodney Refrigerator, "it might just work."

   (b) "Why not try to make the humans stop using him?" asked Rodney Refrigerator. "It might just work."

3. (a) "I want to hear," said Toby. "Just what Rodney has in mind."

   (b) "I want to hear," said Toby, "just what Rodney has in mind."

4. (a) "Okay, here's my plan," said Rodney. "You may not like it, though, because it's going to hurt."

   (b) "Okay, here's my plan," said Rodney, "you may not like it, though, because it's going to hurt."

5. (a) "Don't you think I can be brave," asked Toby? "If your plan will end all my troubles, I'll try it."

   (b) "Don't you think I can be brave?" asked Toby, "if your plan will end all my troubles, I'll try it."

   (c) "Don't you think I can be brave?" asked Toby. "If your plan will end all my troubles, I'll try it."

More Practice

Read the sentences. Decide if they are correctly punctuated and capitalized. In some sentences you must add punctuation or capitalize words. In other sentences you must cross out errors and write the correction above the box.

Example: "Let me hear your plan☒" ☒aid Toby Toaster☐

1. Rodney Refrigerator said☐ "Ⓨou sometimes burn the humans' toast☐"

2. "But then they just use me over again☐" Ⓡeplied Toby Toaster.

3. "My plan is for you to burn the bread often☐" Ⓢaid Rodney☐ "Ⓘf they turn down your heat dial, then you should leave it cold and limp."

4. "How can that Ⓠ" Ⓐsked Toby☐ "Ⓜake my life any easier Ⓠ"

5. Rodney sighed and said☐ ⓊⓉhat Toby really was thinking like a machine.Ⓡ

6. "This is leading Toby into trouble☐" Ⓢnorted Steve Stove⬛ "Ⓘt's only going to make his life worse☐"

7. "I think☐" Ⓢaid Toby☐ "Ⓣhat I'm going to try it anyway☐"

8. "I hear the humans coming down to breakfast☐" Ⓢaid Rodney☐ "Ⓞkay, Toby, make that toast of theirs a mess☐"☐

9. Steve Stove exclaimed☐ "Ⓨou'll be sorry if you do⬛"

Challenge

These sentences have no boxes to help you. Add whatever punctuation is necessary. Where needed, cross out lowercase letters and write capitals above them.

1. Mom, the toaster burned my bread to a crisp said Peter Potter to his mother

2. Peter's mother asked shouldn't you just try another slice of bread with the lever turned down to light

3. This time sighed Peter it didn't even brown the bread

4. It must be broken said Peter's mother if it doesn't work the next time, we'll throw it into the garbage and buy a new one

5. Peter tried again and said that this time it worked perfectly

6. I decided that I'd rather have heartburn said Toby Toaster later to Rodney and Steve than be buried at the dump in a ton of garbage

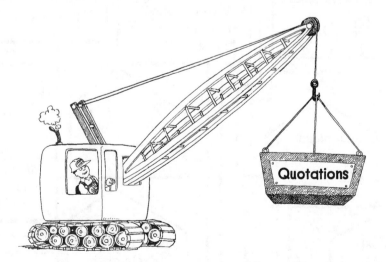

Quotations

Quotations Maze

Complete the maze by following the correct sentences. If a house contains incorrect punctuation or capitalization, stop and go back. You cannot go through that house. The correct path to the finish will take you through ten houses. **Bonus:** What is the total number of houses in the maze that contain correctly written quotations?

"This is my house," said Patrick.

"I don't live here," said Cindy.

"Where," asked Carl, "do you live?"

Emma exclaimed! "I love my cottage."

Miguel said, "my house has two floors."

"Is this house heated?" asked Arthur.

"My roof," said Sari. "Has a hole in it."

Pamela thinks "that her house is pretty."

Tomas asked, "Who lives here?"

"My room," said Traci. "Is upstairs."

"My house is sweet," said Cindy. "I love it."

"This cabin," sighed Maria. "Needs cleaning."

"I live here!" exclaimed Allen.

"My house is tiny," Said the mouse.

"Does my house need painting?" asked Charlotte.

"Do you," asked Aaron, "like this house?"

"This is the wrong house!" yelled Mike.

Karen asked, "Is my house for sale?"

Daniella demanded, "get out of my house!"

"My house is small," Said the dog.

"My house," said Sally, "is at the end of the road."

"The doors of my house," said Tim. "Are locked."

"My house," said Laura, "is on the corner."

"My house blocks the road!" Exclaimed Edwardo.

46 **More on Using Quotation Marks**
Student Page

Sentence Fragments

This Unit Teaches Students

- how to recognize and correct sentence fragments

Getting Started

Students study model sentences that illustrate the idea that a sentence must be a complete thought and then use models as aids to distinguish between complete sentences and fragments. They then work on correcting fragments by (1) adding words to make a complete thought and (2) attaching a fragment to an adjacent complete thought by altering punctuation and capitalization. The exercises tell the story of Maria Mayfair, who is never unhappy.

The unit concludes with two exercises in the form of games—a "secret code" that can be solved only through an understanding of sentence fragments, and a maze where fragments act as blocks on the path to the finish.

Teaching Notes

Sentence fragments are a problem at every level of English instruction because people converse with fragments and often think in fragments. Also, some modern writers use fragments in their work so that students rightly say, "You told us not to use fragments, but look—here's one in the story we're reading." The best response to this observation is something like this: "Sometimes fragments are appropriate; usually they are not. Good writers know when it is okay to use them. When I am sure that you are using sentence fragments purposely and not by mistake, then I'll reconsider."

Students should, of course, be allowed to use fragments when writing dialogue since that is the way people really converse: "When are you leaving?" "On Saturday." "Great!"

Since this unit may be used as self-teaching material, be sure students understand that there may be more than one correct answer to some exercises. For example, when a fragment is to be corrected by adding words, students may find that their additions differ from those in the answer key.

Sentence Fragments

> Maria Mayfair, the happiest girl in Silver City.
>
> Easy to love but hard to understand.
>
> Since nothing seems to upset her.

What's It All About?

Clearly there is something missing in every one of the "sentences" above. While you may be able to work out what is meant, you never find a complete thought. All are examples of a writing problem called **sentence fragments**.

Let's Find Out

The models below give more illustrations of sentence fragments and show ways to correct them.

Models

Sentence Fragment	Sentence
1. Few rainy days for Maria Mayfair.	*There are* few rainy days for Maria Mayfair.
2. Maria, living in her own world of wonders.	Maria *always seems to be* living in her own world of wonders.
3. Reading or making up her own games.	*She enjoys* reading or making up her own games.

Let's Try It

Use the models to help you decide which of the groups of words below are sentences (complete thoughts) and which are sentence fragments (incomplete thoughts). In the spaces provided, write **S** for sentence and **F** for a fragment.

1. Hard for most of us to understand. (   )

2. Someone like Maria Mayfair is hard for us to understand. (   )

3. Nothing upsetting to Maria. (   )

4. Not even nightmares, scrapes, or little brothers? (   )

5. Maria always seems to see the bright side of things. (   )

6. A nightmare for her is a wild adventure. (   )

7. Even when it is full of goblins, gremlins, and imps. (   )

8. Lurking in the doorways, waiting to get her. (   )

9. How can Maria always be so positive and happy? (   )

10. Maybe because she was just born that way. (   )

What Did You Discover?

Sentences 9 and 10 illustrate some of the difficulties in identifying sentence fragments. Sentence 9 is a question and may at first seem to be an incomplete thought since you don't know the answer to the question yet. If a group of words makes a complete question, however, as sentence 9 does, then it is not a fragment.

Sentence 10 presents another problem. It answers the question asked in sentence 9, but words have been left out. They are implied instead of actually stated. So sentence 10 is a fragment. To be a complete thought, it should read, "Maybe *Maria is so happy* because she was just born that way." Or "Maybe she was just born that way." Finally, do not assume that sentence fragments are shorter than full sentences. Sentence 6, a full sentence, is shorter than sentence 7, a sentence fragment.

Let's Practice

There are two ways to correct sentence fragments. You can add words to the fragment to make it a complete thought. Or you can add the fragment to a near-by sentence.

Correcting Sentence Fragments by Adding Words

Decide if each group of words is a sentence or fragment. In the space below each fragment, write a complete sentence by adding the necessary words. Use the model sentences if you need help.

1. One very happy person in Silver City.

_____

2. That person is Maria Mayfair.

_____

3. Always smiling and laughing.

_____

4. Why is she always happy?

_____

5. Because she always makes things fun.

_____

6. Maria making other people smile too.

_____

7. She radiates contentment.

_____

8. And makes life fun for her friends too.

_____

Correcting Sentence Fragments by Combining

Example:

Sentence fragments can be corrected in another way.
By attaching them to a nearby sentence.

Look at the words in italics. Are they a sentence? No, they are a *sentence fragment*. An easy way to correct the problem: replace the period after the word *way* in the sentence before with a comma and make the *b* of *by* lower case.

Corrected fragment:

Sentence fragments can be corrected in another way, by attaching them to a nearby sentence.

Here is another example of a sentence followed by a fragment:

Example:

You will probably like this way of correcting fragments.
Because it is quick and easy.

Corrected fragment:

You will probably like this way of correcting fragments because it is quick and easy.

In both these examples, the fragment was fixed by simply fusing it with the first sentence.

Let's Practice

Read each pair of sentences. Correct any fragments by combining. Be careful—some problems contain two complete sentences and need no correction.

1. Maria Mayfair never seems to be bothered by the weather. Because she always finds a way to make the best of it.

2. She just changes her plans. If it is raining or too icy to go outside.

3. One day she and her friend Monica planned to have a sidewalk sale. And sell all their old books, toys, and games.

4. They had just finished putting all their precious possessions on tables by the street. When the dark clouds overhead suddenly turned into waterfalls.

5. It began to pour. Maria and Monica had no time to gather up their belongings.

6. When Monica started to cry. Maria just laughed and hugged her friend.

7. "Stop that useless crying, Monica. You're just making things wetter."

8. That was a typical Maria Mayfair response. A comment so surprising that it made Monica stop weeping.

9. In fact, Monica had hardly stopped crying. Before she began smiling and giggling.

10. The two girls were soon singing in the rain and playing with their old wet dolls and toys. Turning a disaster into a day they never forgot.

FUN WITH SENTENCE FRAGMENTS

Sentence Fragment Code

Look for sentence fragments in the paragraph below. If you circle the capital letter that begins each fragment, the circled letters will spell out words that form a short sentence.

Rainy days can be fun. Yes, even more fun, sometimes, than sunny ones. On rainy days. You can, for example, turn your home into a castle. As the thunder and lightning rage outside, you imagine yourself a dragon inspector searching for a hidden beast. Under the beds, in the closets, down in the cellar. To protect yourself, you wear your anti-dragon outfit. Designed to repel even the fiercest fire-breather. You carry your special bag of inspection tools. Including your homemade dragon formula, a book about capturing dragons, and a dragon net. You are well prepared for a delicious adventure. Detecting and eliminating the unwelcome visitor in your castle. If dragons are a little too strenuous for you, you may wish to do something else, however. With the hammering rain providing background music. You may just want to stare out into the storm and dream about doing fun things with friends. Especially if you have one very special friend. Last but not least. You may just wish to curl up with an exciting book. Like a mystery or maybe even a ghost story.

With the hammering rain providing background music,

Sentence Fragment Maze

Complete the maze by following the correct sentences. If a box contains a sentence fragment, stop and go back. You cannot go through that box. The correct path to the finish will take you through nine boxes.

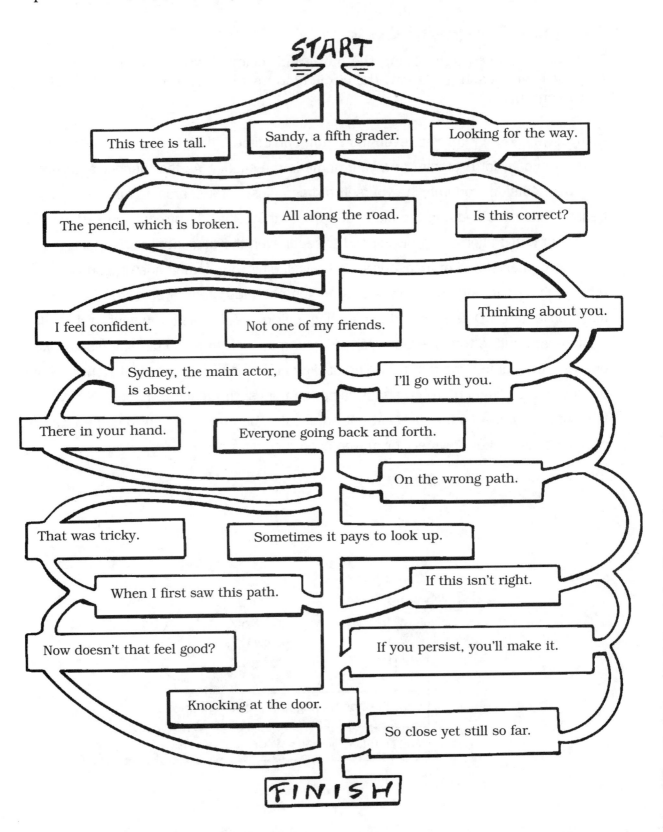

START

This tree is tall.

Sandy, a fifth grader.

Looking for the way.

The pencil, which is broken.

All along the road.

Is this correct?

Thinking about you.

I feel confident.

Not one of my friends.

Sydney, the main actor, is absent.

I'll go with you.

There in your hand.

Everyone going back and forth.

On the wrong path.

That was tricky.

Sometimes it pays to look up.

If this isn't right.

When I first saw this path.

If you persist, you'll make it.

Now doesn't that feel good?

Knocking at the door.

So close yet still so far.

FINISH

Recognizing Run-On Sentences

This Unit Teaches Students

- how to recognize run-on sentences
- how to correct run-on sentences with periods or semicolons

Getting Started

This unit focuses on identifying run-on sentences. By completing exercises based on the theme of tall tales, students learn to recognize when a group of words "run on" with more than one complete thought.

The unit concludes with two exercises in the form of games—a "secret code" that requires a knowledge of run-on sentences and a maze in which run-ons act as blocks on the path to the finish.

Teaching Notes

Since run-ons are a frequent and difficult problem in student writing, you'll find two units devoted to them. This unit points out that run-ons are not necessarily long sentences that run on and on, but two thoughts run together with no punctuation or with only a comma separating them (a "comma splice").

Before handing out the material, you might prepare students by giving a definition of a run-on sentence and then a few examples. Challenge the class: "How short can a run-on sentence be? Can anyone give me one in, say, less than six words?" (Come inside, it's raining. Look, run!)

Recognizing Run-On Sentences

What's It All About?

> Funny stories take many forms, some are subtle and some are very broad.
>
> Tall tales are often very popular, their humor is based on exaggeration.

How many sentences are there in the box? If you said there are really four, not just two, you are right. Each group of words ending in a period is really two sentences, two complete thoughts. If you write two complete thoughts together as if they were one thought, you make the mistake called a **run-on sentence**. This unit will help you find and correct run-on sentences.

Model Sentences

Run-On Sentences	**Corrected Sentences**
1. My room wins the prize for messiness to get to my bed I have to dig a tunnel	My room wins the prize for messiness. **T**o get to my bed I have to dig a tunnel.
2. He can't remember anything, he has to be reminded to take the wrapper off a stick of chewing gum.	He can't remember anything. **H**e has to be reminded to take the wrapper off a stick of chewing gum.
3. Those last two sentences contain exaggerations, they could be part of a tall tale.	Those last two sentences contain exaggerations; **t**hey could be part of a tall tale.

The three examples illustrate **run-on sentences** and two ways of correcting them. As you can see, **a run-on sentence occurs when two (or more) complete thoughts are run together and punctuated as if they were one sentence.**

The first model of a run-on sentence has no punctuation at all between the two complete thoughts. The second model illustrates a more common run-on error. It shows the use of a comma to "splice" together two complete thoughts. This kind of run-on sentence is called a "comma splice."

To correct run-on sentences such as those in models 1 and 2, put a period between the two thoughts. If the ideas are closely related, you may use a semi-colon (;) as shown in the third model. Notice that when you use a semicolon, you do not need to start the second complete thought with a capital letter.

Caution: Long sentences are not necessarily run-on sentences. Some long sentences (like this one) can be correctly punctuated with just commas, while some short sentences can be run-ons.

Short run-on sentence: It's raining, I'm all wet.
Correction: It's raining. I'm all wet.

Let's Try It

Read the sentence pairs. Circle the letter of the one that is correctly punctuated. You may use the model sentences to help you.

1. (a) Henry Whopper was a teller of tall tales, he even told them to his teachers.

(b) Henry Whopper was a teller of tall tales. He even told them to his teachers.

2. (a) One day Ms. Nesbit, the history teacher, asked Henry where his homework was, she should have known better than to ask!

(b) One day Ms. Nesbit, the history teacher, asked Henry where his homework was. She should have known better than to ask!

3. (a) Henry sighed and dropped his eyes. In fact, he seemed almost ready to cry.

(b) Henry sighed and dropped his eyes, in fact, he seemed almost ready to cry.

4. (a) He began, "Well, Ms. Nesbit, I did do my homework, actually, I did it three times."

(b) He began, "Well, Ms. Nesbit, I did do my homework. Actually, I did it three times."

5. (a) "My pet gerbil Godzilla chewed my first copy into tiny pellets. My little sister used the second one to practice her finger painting."

(b) "My pet gerbil Godzilla chewed my first copy into tiny pellets, my little sister used the second one to practice her finger painting "

6. (a) Ms. Nesbit knew Henry well. She also saw his homework paper sticking out of his history book.

(b) Ms. Nesbit knew Henry well she also saw his homework paper sticking out of his history book.

Let's Practice

Read the sentences. Decide if there are any run-ons. Rewrite each run-on sentence so it is correct.

Example: Henry Whopper loved to tell tall tales, you will find an example of one of them below.

Henry Whopper loved to tell tall tales. You will find an example of one of them below.

1. I know I was late getting home, I'm going to tell you why.

2. First, the school bus was late the driver kept pulling into ice-cream stores and buying us all triple-dip cones.

3. I finally got off the bus and started to walk home when that tornado struck.

4. Luckily, I wasn't hurt, it only picked me up and dropped me over at Kareem's house.

5. I know Kareem's house is only five minutes from home I had to help Kareem, however, get rid of all the movie producers.

6. These film people were there, trying to talk me into going straight to Hollywood to make a movie about my trip home from school.

7. You shouldn't be angry about my being late, you should be glad I got here at all.

FUN WITH RUN-ON SENTENCES

Secret Code

You can crack the secret code if you understand run-on sentences well. In the sample paragraph the underlined letters follow run-on errors. Notice that some run-on sentences are incorrectly linked with commas, while other are not. When put together, the underlined letters spell out a word.

Example: It's raining hard you should come inside. You are the only one who hasn't, everyone else came in ten minutes ago. Your clothes are soaking surely you can't be having fun. (*Hidden word: yes.*)

Now it's your turn. Read the tall tale. Underline each letter that follows a run-on error. Then put the letters together to form a short sentence.

We used to have a wreck for a car, you should have seen it. It was a sickly yellow color and completely rusted out, only an expert could tell which were the windows and which were the holes. The top was so rusted that rain poured in, underneath there were just as many holes to let the water run back out again.

In some ways, however, it was a great car, at least that's what we thought. With all those holes we didn't need air conditioning. Also, going in that car made every trip an adventure riding down to the store was just like going on the bump'em cars at the amusement park. The doors rattled and the motor coughed and snorted, even the horn was exciting. We never knew when it would decide for itself to start honking.

I don't know why my father ever sold it, cars that special are hard to come by. You are probably wondering who would ever want to buy it from us lots of people did! Artists, photographers, and museums were bidding for it, even Hollywood studios wanted it. They all said the same thing, very soon this car is going to be famous. No one could believe that a wreck like that could ever make it down the driveway. So the bidding war started, eventually a newcomer, a millionaire Swiss dairy owner, bid so high that everyone else gave up and let him have it. What did he want it for? He uses our old yellow car as a moving advertisement, reportedly he drives it around claiming it's the world's biggest piece of Swiss cheese.

Run-On Sentence Maze

Complete the maze by following the correct sentences. If a box contains a run-on sentence, stop and go back. You cannot go through that box. The correct path to the finish will take you through eight boxes.

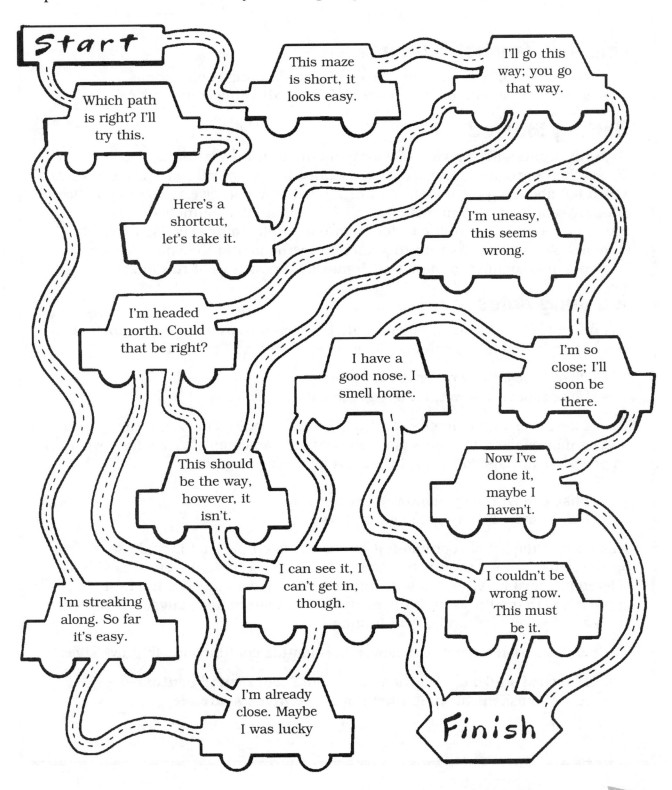

Correcting Run-On Sentences

This Unit Teaches Students

- how to correct run-on sentences with coordinating conjunctions
- how to correct run-on sentences with subordinating conjunctions

Getting Started

The unit begins with a review of concepts taught in the last unit. Model sentences then introduce the use of conjunctions to correct run-ons. The exercises, which tell about a girl who wants to be a great inventor, give students practice in using coordinating conjunctions and subordinating conjunctions to correct run-on sentences. The unit concludes with a proofreading exercise in which students correct run-ons with the different methods that they have learned. Students also complete a maze that tests their knowledge of run-ons.

Teaching Notes

It is difficult for students to differentiate between a coordinating conjunction like *but* or *for* and an adverb like *however* or *therefore*. For example:

- "I like candy, but I never get to eat it."
- "I like candy; however, I never get to eat it."

The easiest explanation to give students is that a conjunction is a *joining word* that cannot be moved from its position between two complete thoughts; whereas an adverb is a transitional word that can be moved around:

- "I like candy; I never, however, get to eat it."
- "I like candy; I never get to eat it, however."

Why doesn't the list of coordinating conjunctions on page 64 include *so*? Speakers use *so* as a conjunction in conversation all the time, but it is still considered informal in writing. If students use *so* as a conjunction, the best approach is to treat it as an issue of style. As an alternative, suggest a sentence such as: "Since I like candy, I eat it often."

You may also wish to point out how subordinating conjunctions improve style:

- "I finished studying, and then I went out." [**compound sentence**]
- "After I finished studying, I went out." [**complex sentence**]

Correcting Run-On Sentences

What's It All About?

The first sentence in the box is a **run-on sentence**. Two ideas have been incorrectly linked with a comma. (This mistake is also called a **comma splice**.) The rest of the sentences in the box illustrate ways to correct this punctuation error. Note: Run-on sentences may not have even a comma between the complete thoughts, and they may be very short:

Abby is clever she is also a dreamer.

1. Abby Armstrong was ambitious, she wanted to be a famous inventor.
2. Abby Armstrong was ambitious. She wanted to be a famous inventor.
3. Abby Armstrong was ambitious; she wanted to be a famous inventor.
4. Abby Armstrong was ambitious, for she wanted to be a famous inventor.
5. Abby Armstrong was ambitious since she wanted to be an inventor.

Correcting Run-On Sentences With Periods

One good way to correct a run-on sentence is to make it two sentences. Read the sentences and decide if they are correct or not. Rewrite any run-ons so that they are two correct sentences.

Example: Abby is clever, she is also a dreamer.

Correction: Abby is clever. She is also a dreamer.

1. Most of Abby Armstrong's ideas for inventions don't work, they are too outrageous.

2. She often gets ideas for things she can't make, for instance, she once wanted to create a combination TV set and microwave oven.

3. Abby thought it would be a great combination, you could pop your microwave popcorn without missing any of your favorite show.

4. Once she took boards and made a chute down her front stairs, she called it a "stairslide."

5. After getting several splinters, she gave up on the stairslide, however.

Correcting Run-On Sentences With Semicolons

When you want to connect two related complete thoughts in one sentence, you can use a semicolon to separate them.

Example:
    Run-on: Semicolons are useful, they can help you relate ideas.
    Semicolon correction: Semicolons are useful; they can help you relate ideas.

Read the "sentences" and decide if they are correct or not. Add a semicolon to correct any run-ons.

1. Abby had a good idea for generating electricity she called it making "exer-tricity."

2. She wanted to attach generators to the exercise machines at her parents' health club so that all those peddling and pumping people would create electrical power as they worked out.

3. The manager of the club thought her idea was excellent he said that generators would be too expensive to install, however.

Correcting Run-On Sentences With Conjunctions

A *junction* is a place where things *join together*, and the prefix *con-* means "with." Thus a **conjunction** is a word that *joins* one part of a sentence *with* another. There are two kinds of conjunctions, **coordinating** and **subordinating**. You can use both kinds to connect the two complete thoughts of a run-on sentence.

A. Using Coordinating Conjunctions to Correct Run-Ons

When you *co*exist, you exist *equally*, and when you *co*operate, you work *together*. **Coordinating conjunctions** make each complete thought in a sentence equal with the others. Study the **coordinating conjunctions** in the box.

and but or nor for yet

Example:
    Run-on sentence: Abby has a vivid imagination, she is also very creative.
    Correction using a coordinating conjunction: Abby has a vivid imagination, **and** she is also very creative.

As this example illustrates, the conjunction **and** joins the two complete thoughts of the run-on sentence. **Important**: Unless the ideas are very short, you must also have a comma after the first complete thought.

Let's Try It

In the following sentences, write in a conjunction to connect the two parts of the run-on sentences.

Example: Abby's inventions often fail, but she never gets discouraged.

1. One of Abby Armstrong's failures was fortunate, it led to a future success.

2. The failure was an invention she first called a page-turner, she later called it a page-ripper.

3. It was made of paper clips attached to a strong spring, it was supposed to turn the page of a book when you pressed it.

4. The spring was so strong that it tore the page in half, the book slammed shut.

5. Abby was not upset, the accident had given her a new idea.

6. She turned the device around and attached it to the covers of the book, now she had a successful invention that kept her book from closing by itself.

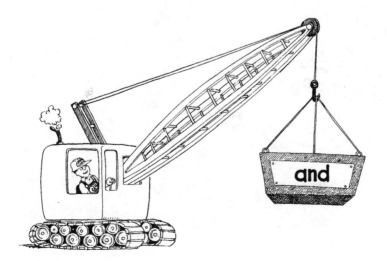

B. Using Subordinating Conjunctions to Correct Run-Ons

When you are in a *sub*marine, you are *under* the ocean, and when your body temperature is *sub*normal, it is *less than* the normal body temperature.

Subordinating conjunctions enable you to put two thoughts together and at the same time make one thought subordinate to, of lesser importance than, the other thought.

Here are two complete thoughts:

- I like pizza. I rarely eat it.
- *Although* I like pizza, I rarely eat it.

Notice the subordinating conjunction *although* in the second sentence. Now the first thought is no longer independent. It has become subordinate to the second complete thought.

Subordinating conjunctions like *although*, *because*, *while*, *before*, and *if* can be used to correct run-on sentences.

Example:

Run-on sentence: Abby Armstrong gets new ideas easily, she often has difficulty making those ideas work.

Correction using a subordinating conjunction: Although Abby Armstrong gets new ideas easily, she often has difficulty making those ideas work.

Let's Try It

In each of the following run-on sentences, there is a blank space. Add a subordinating conjunction to complete each sentence. If you need help, use the list of subordinating conjunctions that follows the sentences.

Example: _____*If*_____ one invention does not work, Abby just thinks up a new one.

1. _____ one of her ideas got her into trouble, Abby still did not get discouraged.

2. One such unfortunate idea came to her one day _____ she was taking a shower.

3. _____ she closed the bathtub drain as she took a shower, then she could save the water and wash her dog Fluffy in it.

4. _____ the bathtub was still not full enough to wash Fluffy, Abby let the shower continue to run as she got dressed.

5. _____ she was downstairs looking for Fluffy, Abby noticed water dripping through the ceiling.

6. Abby's parents did not punish her for the minor flood _____ they liked to encourage her inventive thinking.

Partial List of Subordinating Conjunctions					
after	before	since	unless	when	although
as	if	though	until	while	because

Putting It All Together

Rewrite the following run-on sentences. You can use any of the methods that you have learned to correct the errors.

Example:
    Run-on sentence: Abby is young, she has already invented many things.
    Possible corrections:
    Although Abby is young, she has already invented many things.
    Abby is young; she has already invented many things.

1. Some of Abby's schoolmates laugh at her inventions, they think her projects are silly.

2. Abby knows that she is not the first to be laughed at, many famous inventors were treated with scorn.

3. Robert Fulton built a steamboat in 1807 named the *Clermont*, people made fun of it and called it "Fulton's Folly."

4. Some said the Wright Brothers were wasting their time and money, they were working on a machine that would fly.

5. Abby Armstrong may have the last laugh, she may end up as a famous inventor.

Run-On Sentence Maze

Complete the maze by following the correct sentences. If a box contains a run-on sentence, stop and go back. You cannot go through that box. The correct path to the finish will take you through twelve boxes.

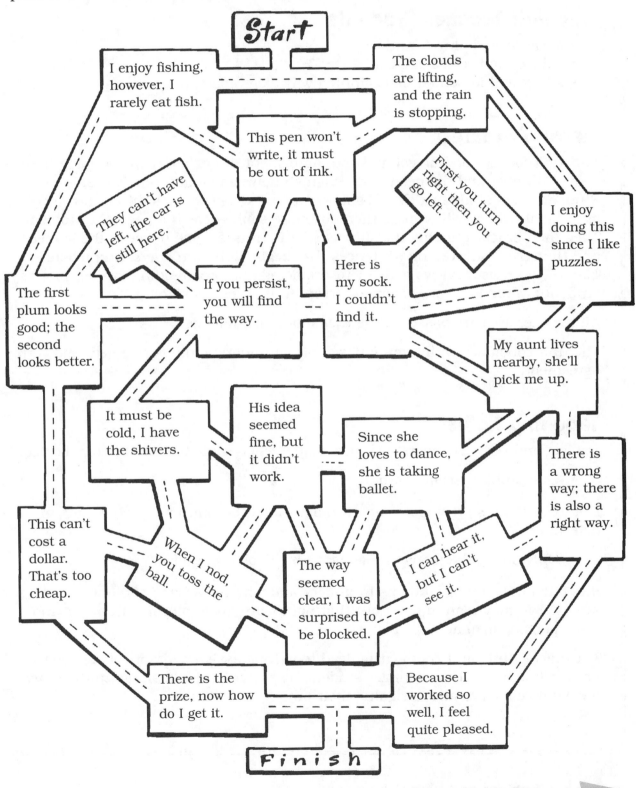

Subject and Verb Agreement

This Unit Teaches Students

- singular and plural number
- subject and verb agreement
- agreement in sentences beginning with *here*, *there*, and *where*

Getting Started

This unit focuses on subject and verb agreement. It begins by introducing the idea of number and the need to distinguish between singular and plural nouns. Students then study models of basic sentences with correct subject and verb agreement, which will prepare them for more sophisticated agreement problems. They then practice finding the subject when phrases come between the subject and the verb, and work on sentences that begin with *here*, *there*, and *where*. The final exercise reviews agreement problems in a proofreading format, just as students would look for agreement errors in their own writing.

All the exercises are based on the theme of fanciful foods.

The unit concludes with a maze based on an understanding of subject and verb agreement.

Teaching Notes

Subject and verb agreement is easier to spot when sentences are uncomplicated:

- "One problem seems hard."

But as sentences grow more complex, agreement becomes more confusing to determine:

- "Only one of the many problems in this book seem hard."

It is often difficult for students to understand why the second sentence needs *seems*. You may wish to point out that nouns are made plural with an *-s*, and third-person singular verbs also end in *-s*.

The story in this unit could easily lead to writing assignments involving food preparation and eating. Younger students especially enjoy making up their own imaginative recipes and designing their own restaurant menus.

Subject and Verb Agreement

> One **hamburger** is a singular subject.
> Two **cheeseburgers** are a plural subject.
> A **hamburger and drink** are a compound subject that is plural.
> **Neither a knife nor a fork** is a compound subject that is singular.

What's It All About?

The box illustrates examples of **number**. Some of the subjects are **singular.** Some are **plural.** You use singular and plural words all the time without thinking about it— you say one *cat* (singular) and three *dogs* (plural). To make most nouns plural, add an *-s* to the singular form of the word: one *dog* becomes two *dogs,* one *house* becomes many *houses.* Some words are exceptions: one *woman* and two *women,* one *child* and two *children,* one *deer* and three *deer,* and one *phenomenon* and many *phenomena.*

The sentences in the opening box illustrate another rule of English grammar: The verb in a sentence must **agree** with its subject in number. This means that when we say *one hamburger,* we use the singular verb form *is,* but when we say *two hamburgers,* we use the plural form *are.*

Let's Try It

In the space after each word write **S** if the word is singular and **P** if the word is plural. (For one word you must write both **S** and **P** because the form does not change.)

birds _____   chair _____   turkey _____   eggs _____   men _____

building _____   moose _____   parties _____   folders _____   idea _____

Model Sentences

Singular	Plural
The hamburger **is** too rare.	The chip**s are** too salty.
The cheeseburger **has** no cheese.	The drink**s have** no fizz.
The phone **does** not work.	The ice machine**s do** not freeze.
This cafe **needs** a new manager.	The patron**s need** their money back.

As the model sentences show, the singular form of a verb ends in -*s* when the subject is a singular noun or pronoun— *he, she,* or *it.* Examples: One dog run**s**. He run**s**.

Notice that when the subject is plural, the verb form often does not end in -*s.* Examples: Two dog**s** run. They run.

Let's Try It

Underline the correct form of the verb:

1. The Daft Cafe (is, are) not everyone's favorite place to eat.

2. The meals (has, have) been known to be very exotic.

3. The chef there (likes, like) to try out new dishes such as "seaweed surprise."

4. He (doesn't, don't) seem to care if no one orders his creations.

5. Some daring customers only (orders, order) the chef's spicy specials like his "fire ant appetizer" or his "searing sardine soufflé."

FINDING THE CORRECT SUBJECT

Sometimes agreement mistakes occur because the subject and verb are separated. **For example:**

Incorrect: The salad with red and green peppers **are** very spicy.

The verb here should be *is* because the subject of the sentence is *salad,* not *peppers.*

Study the model sentences on page 73. The subject and verb are underlined. The phrases that separate the subject and verb are written in boldface type.

Model Sentences

The <u>cost</u> **of most of the main courses** <u>is</u> very moderate.

The <u>prices</u> **of the items at the salad bar** <u>are</u> very low.

This <u>menu</u>, **filled with so many oddities**, <u>gives</u> some people a start.

Although *courses* in the first model sentence is plural, it is not the subject. *Courses* is part of a phrase. The real subject is the singular word *cost,* which takes a singular verb form. You can figure out which word is the subject by carefully asking yourself what particular thing or person the verb is referring to. In the second model sentence, for example, you would ask, "What are very low—the prices or the salad bar?"

Let's Try It

Underline the correct form of the verb.

1. Many dishes at the Daft Cafe (is, are) not crowd-pleasers.

2. For example, a mixture of okra and Brussels sprouts (is, are) not one of the most popular side dishes.

3. The caviar-flavored peaches and pears (does, do) not sell well either.

4. Not one of my friends (like, likes) the eggplant ice cream.

5. But the chef, caring more about creativity than customers, (keeps, keep) turning out strange creations.

6. (Is, Are) one of the people here hungry?

HERE, THERE, AND WHERE

When sentences begin with *here*, *there*, or *where*, agreement problems sometimes occur because the subject follows the verb.

Model Sentences

Incorrect

Here is the mangoes.

There's my crab cakes.

Where's the cookies?

Correct

Here are the mangoes.

There are my crab cakes.

Where are the cookies?

Remember that the contractions *there's*, *here's*, and *where's* stand for "there is," "here is," and "where is."

Let's Try It

Underline the correct form of the verb.

1. (Where is, Where are) the chocolate-covered grasshoppers?

2. (There's, There are) your poached pollywogs.

3. (Here's, Here are) the chef's nose clips.

Putting It All Together

Read the sentences. Cross out incorrect words, and write the correct form in the space above. Be careful: Two of the sentences have no errors.

1. Surprisingly, many people goes to the Daft Cafe.

2. There is actually many reasons for trying it.

3. For one, the menu with all its strange dishes are always amusing.

4. The food with all its strange ingredients makes people talk and laugh together.

5. Also, many dishes, like braised broccoli, is actually good for you.

6. Good for you or not, a salad of turnips, raw spinach, and dandelion greens do not get many takers.

7. There's not many orders for the chef's high-protein earthworm omelet, either.

8. Maybe your school lunch, even with all its problems, sounds better to you than the food at the Daft Cafe.

Agreement Maze

Complete the maze by following the sentences that are correct. If a box contains incorrect agreement, stop and go back. You cannot go through that box. The correct path to the finish will take you through ten boxes.

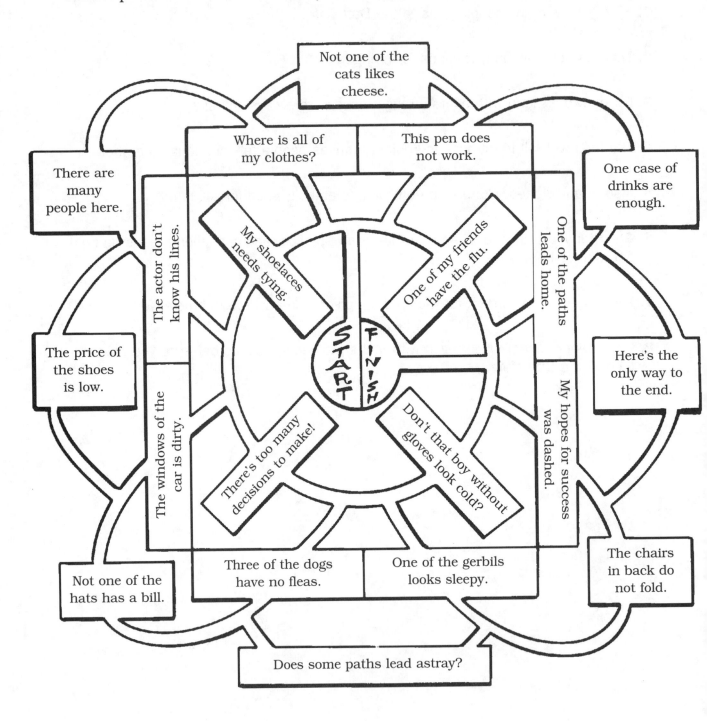

More Subject and Verb Agreement

This Unit Teaches Students

- subject and verb agreement with compound subjects
- subject and verb agreement with indefinite pronoun subjects

Getting Started

Model sentences explain compound subjects. Students also learn that when singular subjects are connected by *or* or *nor*, the verb must be singular. Three types of indefinite pronouns are introduced: those that are always singular, those that are always plural, and those that may be either singular or plural. A suggestion to help students memorize the troublesome singular pronouns is also given. Students complete exercises to practice what they have learned.

The story that runs through the unit is a speculation about the source of eerie noises and lights in the night sky.

Further review is provided in a maze where knowledge of agreement is needed in order to find the right path to the finish.

Teaching Notes

This unit continues the focus on subject/verb agreement introduced in the last unit. Some students will find the work on singular indefinite pronouns to be difficult. When the right form sounds more awkward to students than the incorrect form, they may need extra explanation and help. This might also be a good time to discuss the difference between standard written English and informal English.

When doing the section on the use of *or* and *nor*, students may ask what verb to use if one subject is singular and the other is plural. Though awkward, agreement with the nearer subject is acceptable: "Neither the girls nor Tom is ready."

More Subject and Verb Agreement

Green **lights**, white **streamers**, and electronic **noises are** coming from the night sky.

Both **Stephan** and **Megan are** sure about having witnessed something truly strange.

Neither **Marcella** nor **Sean is** convinced of any unusual occurrence.

What's It All About?

As you can see in the box above, sometimes a verb has two or more subjects in the same sentence. These are called **compound subjects** and are usually connected by the words *and, or,* or *nor.* These joining words are called ***conjunctions.*** Usually a compound subject calls for a plural verb form. But look at the last sentence. Even though there are two subjects—Marcella, Sean—the verb *is* in this sentence is singular.

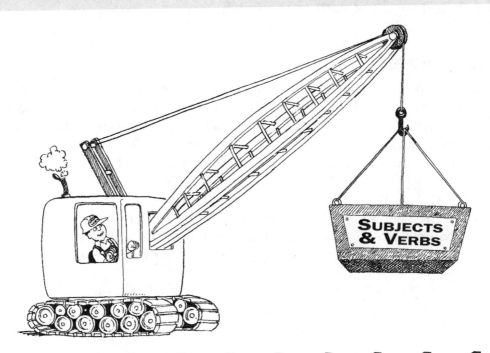

Model Sentences

Plural Compound

Marcia and Morris are nervous.

Both Sarah and he are surprised.

Singular Compound

Sammy or Cindy is the one to ask.

Neither she nor Tomas is sure.

As you can see, if the word connecting a compound subject is *and,* the verb is plural. If the word connecting the compound subject is *or* or *nor,* then the verb is singular. The verb is agreeing with one subject at a time and not with both of them at once. Of course, if *or* or *nor* connect plural subjects like *boys or girls,* then the verb is plural:

Correct: Neither Marcella nor Sean **is** sure what happened.

Also Correct: *Neither the boy**s** nor the girl**s** **are** certain.*

Let's Try It

Underline the correct form of the verb:

1. Both Stephan and Megan (is, are) somewhat frightened about those flashing lights and that eerie noise.

2. Neither Sean nor Marcella (believes, believe) their story.

3. Megan's father, mother, brother, and sister (does, do) trust her tale.

4. Both the pulsing lights in the sky and the weird noises in the distance (was, were) enough to convince Stephan that something bizarre occurred.

5. Maybe an earthquake or even a volcano (was, were) in the making.

INDEFINITE PRONOUNS AS SUBJECTS

Singular	Plural	Singular or Plural
each, either, neither, one,	both	all, any
anyone, everyone,	few	most
someone, anybody,	many	none
everybody, somebody	several	some

The words on the previous page are called **indefinite pronouns**. The ones in the group labeled *singular* often cause agreement problems when they are used as the subject of a sentence.

Model Sentences

Singular

Each of the noises **was** harsh.
Each was also eerie.
Everyone was astounded by the occurrence.
Every one of the onlookers **was** nervous.

Plural

Both of the children **are** certain of their impressions.
Several of the witnesses **are** still doubtful.

Singular or Plural

Some of the story has been exaggerated.
Some of the details have been questioned.

These model sentences illustrate the use of some indefinite pronouns. Don't be confused when a phrase comes between a pronoun and the verb:

• "Each of the noises was harsh."

Although the plural word *noises* is next to the verb, the subject is *Each*, a singular pronoun. The verb is singular too.

If you have studied prepositional phrases, you will have an easier time sorting out which word is the subject. The subject of a sentence is never in a prepositional phrase. Notice that these prepositional phrases often begin with the word *of*.

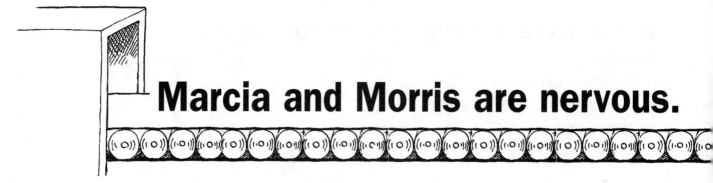

Marcia and Morris are nervous.

Let's Try It

Underline the correct form of the verb.

<u>Helpful</u> <u>hint</u>: Since you usually will not make mistakes with indefinite pronouns, you only have to remember the list of singular words that do cause problems. And you can reduce that list to these four words: *each, either, one, body. Either* reminds you of its negative *neither,* and *one* and *body* stand for all the words that include them (*everyone, everybody, etc.*).

1. One of the witnesses (is, are) sure of seeing sweeping green lights.

2. Many of them (is, are) also sure of hearing loud, howling noises.

3. Each of the onlookers (remembers, remember) the incident differently.

4. Anybody (is, are) welcome to try to explain it.

5. Every one of Stephan's friends (wants, want) his story to be true.

6. Several of them (has, have) even wished that something even more bizarre would happen.

7. All of the authorities (says, say) that there wasn't any special occurrence that night.

8. Somebody (has, have) to be right!

9. (Is, Are) not one person able to find out what really happened?

Sammy or Cindy is the one to ask.

Putting It All Together

The verbs in the following sentences are underlined. Decide if each verb agrees with its subject. Cross out the incorrect verb forms, and write in the correct forms above them.

Example: Some of the sentences below ~~contains~~ clues about that night.

contain

1. Both Doris and Janessa <u>is</u> excited about the big rock concert.

2. Every one of the bands <u>are</u> loud, modern, and weird.

3. Each of them <u>performs</u> on an open stage in the park.

4. Neither Kim nor Ty <u>understand</u> how the light shows work.

5. The lasers and strobe lights <u>produces</u> pulses of green light and swirling white streamers on the clouds overhead.

Challenge

These sentences have no underlined verbs. Find the verbs and decide if they are correct or not. Cross out the incorrect verbs and write in the correct form above.

1. Not one of the people at the concert believe something strange occurred that night.

2. Either a rock concert or a strange occurrence were responsible for the lights and noises that night.

3. Do each of the students here remember that night clearly?

Agreement Maze

Complete the maze by following the correct sentences. If a box contains incorrect agreement, stop and go back. You cannot go through that box. The shortest path to the finish will take you through fourteen boxes. (Some correct boxes do not lead directly to the finish.)

Bonus: How many correct sentences are there in all?

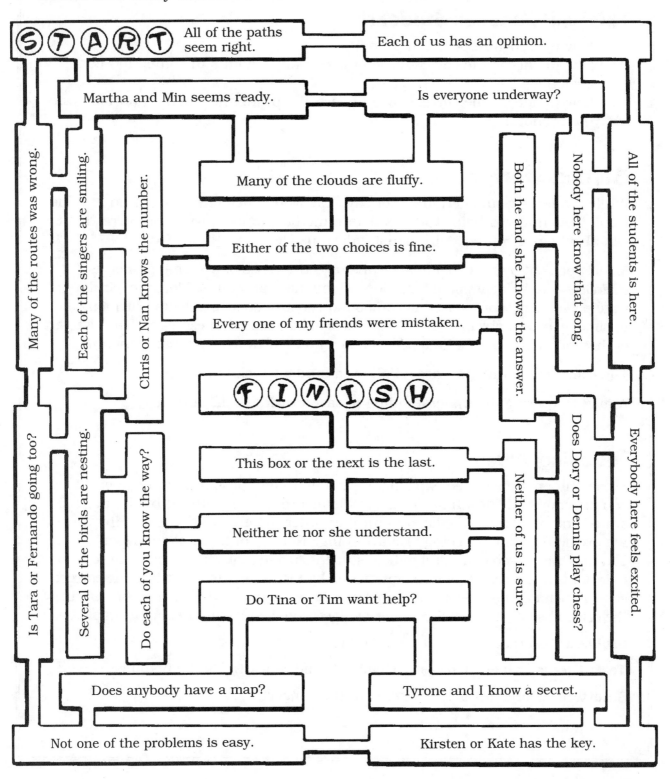

START — All of the paths seem right. | Each of us has an opinion.

Martha and Min seems ready. | Is everyone underway?

Many of the routes was wrong.

Each of the singers are smiling.

Chris or Nan knows the number.

Both he and she knows the answer.

Nobody here know that song.

All of the students is here.

Many of the clouds are fluffy.

Either of the two choices is fine.

Every one of my friends were mistaken.

FINISH

This box or the next is the last.

Neither he nor she understand.

Do Tina or Tim want help?

Is Tara or Fernando going too?

Several of the birds are nesting.

Do each of you know the way?

Neither of us is sure.

Does Dory or Dennis play chess?

Everybody here feels excited.

Does anybody have a map? | Tyrone and I know a secret.

Not one of the problems is easy. | Kirsten or Kate has the key.

Personal Pronouns

This Unit Teaches Students

- how to recognize personal pronouns
- how to choose the correct case of personal pronouns in compound constructions
- how to choose the correct case of personal pronouns when a noun follows the pronoun

Getting Started

While students would certainly not say, "Me won," they often say, "Don and me won!" This unit will help students determine how to use pronouns correctly. It will also help them recognize nonstandard usage.

Models present both the nominative and objective cases of personal pronouns. Exercises give students practice in identifying these pronouns. More models illustrate personal pronouns used in compound constructions. Students learn a method to simplify case problems. They then practice this method in exercises. The last part of the unit discusses what happens when a noun follows a personal pronoun.

The exercises in this unit are all about a student rock band.

A maze requiring the understanding of case provides a final review.

Teaching Notes

Some students may need extra help learning to test pronouns in compound constructions one at a time. Their problems are usually caused by the need to adjust the verb from singular to plural in order to perform the test: "Him and me are going. Him are going? He are going? Neither of them sound right!"
You may wish to do extra drill to help students make that verb adjustment to *is* and to lock in the procedure of trying pronouns by themselves to determine the correct case. Explain that students will sometimes have to change the form of the verb in the original sentence to make a plural subject into a singular one. For example:

Problem: "Gloria and *her* (?) are going to the concert."

Test: "*Her* **is** (rather than *her* **are**) going to the concert." No, it should be *she is.*

Solution: "Gloria and *she* are going to the concert."

Personal Pronouns

Gloria Goosebumps plays the guitar.

Me play the drums.

Gloria and me are looking for a bass player to form a band.

—Danny Drummond

What's It All About?

When Danny Drummond needed a bass player for his band, he put up a poster at school. Did you notice that Danny should have said "I play the drums." not "Me play the drums." Did you also notice Danny's other mistake? He chose the wrong **pronoun** in his third sentence. He should have said, "Gloria and I are looking for a bass player to form a band."

Let's Find Out

Like Danny, you use **personal pronouns** all the time. Here is a list of them in two of their forms.

Personal Pronoun Models

Nominative Case		Objective Case	
Singular	**Plural**	**Singular**	**Plural**
I	we	me	us
you	you	you	you
he, she, it	they	him, her, it	them

Let's Try It

Underline the personal pronouns in the following sentences.
Use the models if you need help.

1. We heard him and you singing.

2. I thought that she sang like a bird.

3. Danny and I thought she sang like a seagull.

4. Gloria did not have kind words for me or for you.

5. She gave us an ugly look, but I only smiled at Gloria and them.

Model Sentences

Incorrect	Correct
1. Gloria and *him* play musical instruments.	**Gloria and *he*** play musical instruments.
2. *Him* and *her* have fun playing hit songs.	***He* and *she*** have fun playing hit songs.
3. The teachers and *us* sometimes sing along.	**The teachers and *we*** sometimes sing along.
4. The teachers and *them* don't always like the same songs.	**The teachers and *they*** don't always like the same songs.
5. James and *me* are going to try out for the band.	**James and *I*** are going to try out for the band.
6. Gloria and Danny may not choose **James or *I*.**	Gloria and Danny may not choose **James or *me*.**
7. They are thinking about **Patricia, Doug, and *we*.**	They are thinking about **Patricia, Doug, and *us*.**

The form of the **personal pronoun** that you use in a sentence depends on how you use it. When a pronoun is the subject of a sentence, use the **nominative case**. When a pronoun is the object of a verb or preposition (models 6 and 7), use the **objective case**. The pronoun *you* doesn't change its form.

Let's Try It

Read each pair of sentences. Underline the correct pronouns. The correct pronoun in the first sentence will be a clue to the correct choice in the second sentence.

1. (He, Him) is composing original songs.
   Gloria and (he, him) are composing original songs.

2. Their songs may not appeal to (we, us).
   Their songs may not appeal to you or (we, us).

3. One song is called "(He, Him) Gives (I, Me) Hives."
   One song is called "His Brother and (He, Him) Give (I, Me) Hives."

4. Another one is titled "Why Can't You Love (I, Me)?"
   Another one is titled "Why Can't You Love My Gerbil and (I, Me)?"

5. Are (us, we) being too critical of the songs?
   Are (us, we) and (they, them) being too critical of the songs?

How To Choose the Correct Case

Since mistakes usually occur when pronouns are part of a compound subject or object, you can test your pronoun choice by simplifying the sentence. Read the sentence with the pronoun by itself.

Sample problem: "The teachers and *them* (?) will be there."

Test: Try the sentence without the words *the teachers and.* "*Them* (?) will be there." No, it should be "*They* will be there."

Solution: "The teachers and *they* will be there."

Let's Try It

Underline the correct form of the personal pronouns in the following sentences. Use the test described on page 87 to help you.

1. Danny Drummond is writing a new song for Hilda and (I, me).

2. (She, Her) and (I, me) don't know how good the song will be.

3. This is the song's title: "You and (She, Her) Turn My Heart to Mush."

4. All our classmates and (we, us) are going to hear Danny, Gloria, and their new band play at lunch.

5. (They, Them) and their band are playing in the gym.

6. Danny and (she, her) are going to dedicate a new song to the teachers and (we, us).

7. The song has a long name: "The Band, Gloria, and (I, Me) Are Feeling as Blue as Blue Jays in Blue Jeans."

More Models

Incorrect	Correct
1. Us students find the band amusing.	**We** students find the band amusing.
2. They often make **we** students laugh.	They often make **us** students laugh.

Sometimes a pronoun is linked with a noun as in the models above. Try the pronoun by itself in the sentence, without the noun.

Sample problem: "Shall *us* (?) girls go hear the band?"

Test: Try the sentence without the word *girls.* "Shall *us* (?)go hear the band?"

No, it should be "Shall *we* go hear the band."

Solution: "Shall *we* girls go hear the band?"

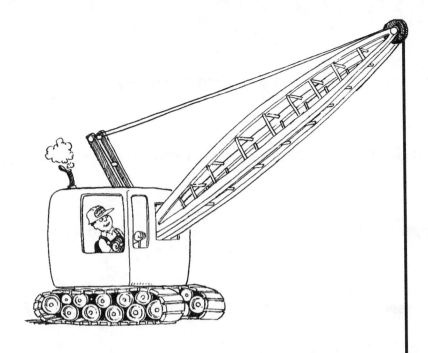

Let's Try It

Underline the correct form of the personal
pronouns in the following sentences.
Use the test to help you.

1. Do Danny and Gloria appeal to (we, us) boys?

2. Are (we, us) seventh graders invited to the dance?

3. The music is too loud and raucous for (we, us) teachers.

Putting It All Together

Read the sentences. Decide if each underlined
pronoun is correct. If a pronoun is incorrect, cross
it out and write in the correct form above it.

1. A hot rumor just reached the ears of <u>we</u> students in the seventh grade.

2. Are Gloria, Danny, and <u>them</u> really going to break up their band?

3. Barbara and <u>me</u> heard that Gloria and <u>they</u> were going to disband.

4. That doesn't sound right to <u>us</u> students who know Gloria and <u>they</u>.

5. Danny and <u>her</u> have been working together too long to stop now.

6. Supposedly it was Danny's song "My Gerbil and <u>Me</u> Belong to <u>She</u> Not You" that is causing Gloria and <u>he</u> to break up.

Challenge

In these sentences the pronouns are not underlined. Find the pronouns and correct any errors.

1. My friends and I would hate to have Gloria and he stop writing songs.

2. The band and they have given my friends and I so many laughs this year!

3. Danny has quashed the rumor with a new song: "Gloria Means More to My Gerbil and I Than Pizza Pie."

Case Maze

Complete the maze by following the correct sentences. If a box contains a pronoun in an incorrect case, stop and go back. You cannot go through that box. The correct path to the finish will take you through seventeen boxes.

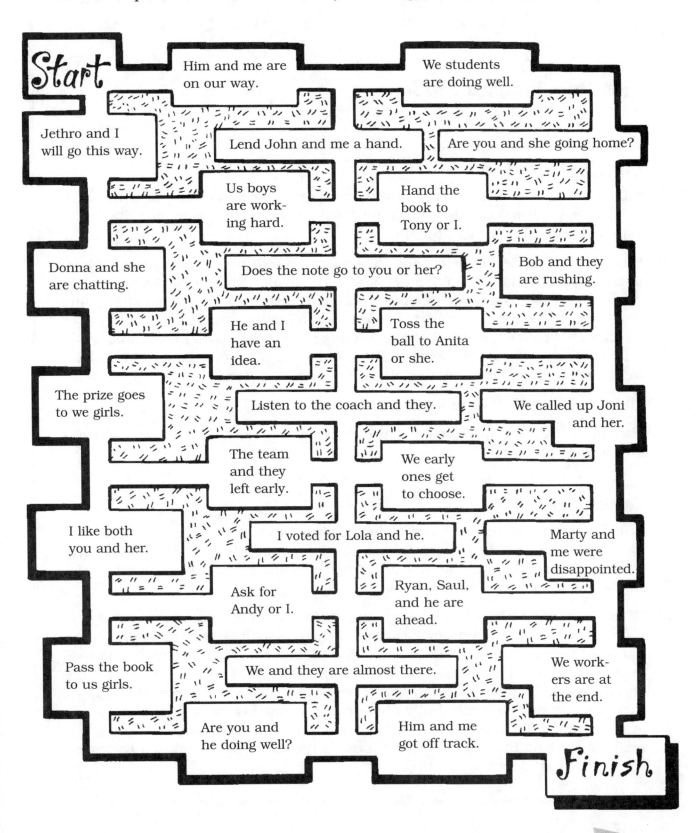

Start

Him and me are on our way.

We students are doing well.

Jethro and I will go this way.

Lend John and me a hand.

Are you and she going home?

Us boys are working hard.

Hand the book to Tony or I.

Donna and she are chatting.

Does the note go to you or her?

Bob and they are rushing.

He and I have an idea.

Toss the ball to Anita or she.

The prize goes to we girls.

Listen to the coach and they.

We called up Joni and her.

The team and they left early.

We early ones get to choose.

I like both you and her.

I voted for Lola and he.

Marty and me were disappointed.

Ask for Andy or I.

Ryan, Saul, and he are ahead.

Pass the book to us girls.

We and they are almost there.

We workers are at the end.

Are you and he doing well?

Him and me got off track.

Finish

Apostrophes in Contractions

This Unit Teaches Students

• how to use apostrophes correctly in contractions

Getting Started

This unit has two sections. The first part presents the procedure for using apostrophes in contractions; the second part isolates several contractions that are especially troublesome for students.

Students use models to determine the correct procedure for using apostrophes in contractions and to help them choose correctly spelled contractions in a practice exercise. A second set of models illustrates the correct form of *let's* and *won't* and also alerts students to the problem of writing *should of* (*should've*) instead of *should have*. After a brief discussion of these special problems, the final exercises review the concepts of the unit, and students practice proofreading for contraction errors as they would in their own stories.

The exercises are all about a girl who has writer's block.

The unit concludes with a maze that uses incorrect contraction forms as blocks on the path to the finish.

Teaching Notes

Students often become confused about apostrophes because they are used both for contractions and for the possessive case of nouns. Also, personal pronouns in the possessive case do not use apostrophes, leading to the widespread confusion of *its* and *it's* and errors like *her's*.

Because apostrophes create such confusion, you will find three units devoted to them. Students move from the easier problems—placing apostrophes in contractions—to the difficult problem of homophones. You can tailor the use of these units to your particular class as well as to the individual students in your class. You may wish to take things slowly, working with your entire group through this unit, letting confidence build about contractions before moving on to possessives in the next unit. On the other hand, you may have students who are ready to work on their own. You can preview the material to work out the right "fit" for your students.

Apostrophes in Contractions

Mindy wrote her teacher a note at the end of her story:

I just cant remember when and where to put in apostrophes. I know I should'nt forget. But who can blame me when English is so confusing?

What's It All About?

Did you notice that Mindy has trouble with **apostrophes?** What two mistakes did she make in her note? Both of Mindy's mistakes are in the use of **contractions.** A contraction is two words put together so that they make a shortened form—"I *can't* remember" instead of "*can not* remember." You don't have to think about apostrophes when speaking, but when writing contractions you do.

Let's Find Out

The models below show the correct use of apostrophes in some common contractions.

Models

Two Words	Contraction
are not	aren't
does not	doesn't
she will	she'll
I have	I've

Aren't she'll won't I've

What Have You Discovered?

Use the models to decide which statement below expresses the rule for where you should put an apostrophe in a contraction. Circle the correct statement of the rule.

1. In a contraction you put an apostrophe where words have been joined together. (*does not* becomes *does'nt*)

2. In a contraction you put an apostrophe where a letter or letters have been left out. (*does not* becomes *doesn't*)

Let's Practice

In the sentences below, underline the correctly spelled contraction. Use the rule and the models to help you.

1. "(I'm, Im) afraid that you look worried. (Whats, What's) wrong, dear?" said Shirley's mother to her daughter.

2. "I have a story to write for English, and I (ca'nt, can't) think of anything to write about," Shirley sighed.

3. "(Did'nt, Didn't) you just write a good story about talking flowers?" asked her mother.

4. Shirley said, "Yes, but I (dont, don't) want to do the same thing twice."

5. "Well, (you've, youve) got a great imagination and (shouldn't, should'nt) worry too much. (Youll, You'll) come up with something," said her mother reassuringly.

6. (Ive, I've) been trying for an hour! So far I (haven't, have'nt) come up with anything better than a pencil that refuses to write, and (thats, that's) boring," Shirley said.

Special Models

Two Words	Correct Contraction	Frequent Error
I would	I'd	I'ld
will not	won't	wont
let us	let's	lets
should have	should've	should of

It is sometimes hard to remember how many letters have been omitted in a contraction. The models show some common errors.

Won't does not fit the usual contraction pattern. Can you see why? The contraction *let's*—as in "*let's go!*"—is easily confused with *lets*, the verb form—*He lets me eat candy.* To test whether you need an apostrophe, try out the two words *let us* for the word *let's* in your sentence.

Example: "Billy *let's* or *lets* his dog sleep on his bed."

Test: "Billy "let us" his dog sleep on his bed." No. Then it should be *lets*, not the contraction.

Solution: "Billy *lets* his dog sleep on his bed."

Also, don't misuse *should **of*** for *should **have*** or *would **of*** for *would **have***.

Let's Try It

Read the sentences. Decide if each underlined word is correct. If it is wrong, cross it out and write the correct form above.

Example: I w~~on~~t wear any of these dresses.
(correction above: won't)

1. "<u>Lets</u> see if I can help you find a writing topic," said Shirley's mother.

2. "Thanks, Mom. <u>I'd</u> <u>of</u> asked you before, but I <u>did'nt</u> want to bother you,"

said Shirley.

3. Shirley's mother said, "<u>Ive</u> just finished reading an article that says that *but-*

terflies should really be called *flutterbys*. <u>Would'nt</u> that be a good subject?"

4. "I probably would <u>of</u> said yes if I <u>hadn't</u> already written a story about a

contrary caterpillar that <u>wont</u> turn into a butterfly," said Shirley.

5. Shirley's mother laughed and said, "I <u>didn't</u> read that one.

It must <u>of</u> been funny.

Challenge

The contractions in these sentences are not underlined. Find the errors, cross them out, and write the corrections in above. Some sentences have more than one error.

1. Shirley sighed and said, "I wish I had'nt already written about the bulldozer who fell in love. Thats my favorite story idea."

2. "I think youve got a problem, but I've got an idea," said Shirley's mother.

3. "I would'nt be surprised," added her mother, "if you dont find a topic in five minutes. Lets take a walk around the house."

4. "Whats the point of that? I don't get it," said Shirley.

5. Her mother said, "If we just walk slowly, Ill bet you'll see something that will inspire you."

6. "I'm sorry, mom," Shirley said, "but I do'nt think Ill see anything thats new or fresh."

7. "Maybe you wont," said her mother, "but lets try anyway."

8. "Heres the living room," said Shirley's mother. "Now just pretend that you've never seen this room before."

9. "Okay," said Shirley, "but I should of just stayed upstairs and—"

10. "Whats the matter?" asked her mother.

11. "I've never really looked at that mirror on the wall before!" whispered Shirley. "Does'nt it look like a passage into another room? Bye, Mom—and thanks!"

**Apostrophes in Contractions
Student Page**

Contraction Maze

Complete the maze by following the correct contractions. When you come to a word that is incorrect, stop and go back. You cannot go through that word. The right path to the finish goes through eleven correctly spelled contractions.

Bonus question: How many correctly spelled words are there in the entire maze, including the words **start** and **finish**?

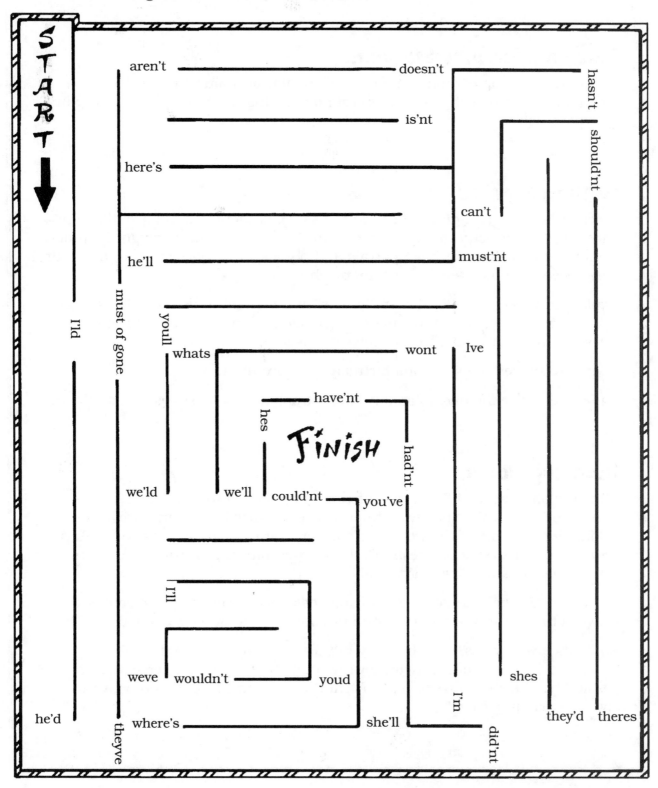

Apostrophes in Possessives

This Unit Teaches Students

- how to use apostrophes in forming singular and plural possessives
- how to distinguish between plural nouns, singular possessives, and plural possessives

Getting Started

Since *girls, girl's,* and *girls'* all sound the same, students often have difficulty choosing the correct form of the word. This unit leads them through the problem of distinguishing between plurals and possessives—both singular and plural possessives—with a step-by-step approach.

Explanatory material provides students with a method to test whether a word is a plural or a possessive. Students study models of singular and plural possessives and then formulate the rules for themselves.

The exercises tell the story of a birthday treasure hunt.

A maze requiring the understanding of apostrophes in possessives reviews the unit.

Teaching Notes

Students often have difficulty in differentiating among words such as *birds, bird's,* and *birds'*. You may wish to provide extra drill as the unit progresses, asking, for example, if the word *bird's* in "one *bird's* beak" is possessive. And how about, "The *birds* are nesting"? Then when plural possessives come up, you can add phrases like "two *birds'* tails."

You might also help students identifying possessive forms when adjectives come between the possessive and the noun it modifies—the bird's *gaping, orange* beak.

Students love rhymes, and the story in this unit may provide them with writing ideas. You might even ask them to write a tale that combines verse and prose. A possibility: The enchantress said: "From this moment, from this time, you will always speak in rhyme."

Apostrophes in Possessives

The artists work in the schools art rooms . . .

What's It All About?

Is this the start of a sentence telling about many artists working in many schools' art rooms? Or is it the beginning of a sentence about many artists working in one school's art rooms? Without apostrophes, you can't be sure.

Let's Find Out

Apostrophes are useful to us, for they make sentences clear. The models below show the correct spelling of plurals and singular possessives.

Models

Plural Noun
boys (two or more boys)
stories (two or more stories)
bosses (two or more bosses)

Singular Possessive
boy's (one boy's hat)
story's (one story's title)
boss's (one boss's desk)

DID YOU KNOW?

Apostrophes used for possessives came into the English language as a mistake. In the late seventeenth century, scholars believed incorrectly that the -s ending used for the possessive case of nouns was a contraction of the word his. They thought, for example, that the boys hat was a contraction of the boy his hat, and they insisted that an apostrophe be inserted to show that the letters hi- had been omitted. From then on the "correct" spelling became the boy's hat.

Why do apostrophes cause so many spelling problems? If you say the pairs of model words aloud, the reason should be clear. Do you hear any difference between *stories* and *story's*? The words sound the same, but they are spelled differently. If you can't hear a difference, then it is easy to write the wrong form of the word.

How can you tell when you should use an apostrophe? Look carefully at your sentence when you are unsure about a word ending in -s, and ask yourself these questions.

- Does the word mean **plural**, the idea of **more than one**?
- Or does it mean **possessive**, the idea of **belonging to**?

Example 1: Two (dogs, dog's) were playing with a cat.

Ask the question: **More than one** dog or **something belonging to** a dog?

Answer: More than one dog. Use *dogs* (the plural form).

Example 2: Two dogs were playing with a (cats, cat's) toy.

Ask the question: **More than one** cat or **something belonging to** a cat?

Answer: A toy **belonging to** a cat. Use *cat's* (the possessive form).

Be careful: You also often show possession by using a phrase starting with *of*, and then you need no apostrophe. **Example:** *The cat's paws* could also be expressed as *the paws of the cat. Paws* is plural, not possessive, in both of these cases and does not need an apostrophe.

Let's Try It

Underline the correct form of the word.

1. (Miguels, Miguel's) birthday party was held in the park, and his excited (friends, friend's) opened the first clue of a treasure hunt.

2. "The (trees, tree's) in the park

Are not all of one size.

Search one huge (trees, tree's) bark

For the way to the prize."

3. "That oak (trees, tree's) top (branches, branch's) reach up higher than all the rest," whispered Rafi to his partner Kevin.

4. Min and Marcia had already started running towards the stand of (trees, tree's) at the (parks, park's) edge.

5. The two other (groups, group's) quickly spotted that particular (oaks, oak's) height and ran after their (classmates, classmate's).

More Models

Regular Plural Noun	Regular Singular Possessive	Regular Plural Possessive
1) two **boys**	one **boy's** hats	two **boys'** hats
2) two **stories**	one **story's** title	two **stories'** titles
3) two **bosses**	one **boss's** desk	two **bosses'** desks

Look at the first line of models. Those four letters b-o-y-s have been been spelled three different ways. The placement of the apostrophe makes a big difference in the meaning of the word. For example, The teacher couldn't find the boys hats. How many boys are involved? Only one boy who has lost more than one hat? Or several boys who have lost their hats? Without an apostrophe, you can't be sure.

What Did You Discover?

Circle the correct statements. Use the models on page 99 to help you.

1. (a) To make a regular singular possessive, add -'s to the singular word.

(b) To make a regular singular possessive, add -s' to the singular word.

2. (a) To make a regular plural possessive, add -'s to the singular word.

(b) To make a regular plural possessive, write the plural word and then add an apostrophe.

Exception

As so often happens in English, there is an exception to the rule for making plural possessives. Words like woman, child, and deer, which do not add -s to make their plurals, do not just add an apostrophe to make their plural possessive.

Model of a Noun with an Irregular Plural

Singular	Irregular Plural	Singular Possessive	Irregular Plural Possessive
one woman	two women	one woman's hats	two women's hats

Let's Try It

Circle the correct statement of the rule for making an irregular plural possessive.

(a) To make an irregular plural possessive, add -s' to the plural form of the word.
(child—children—children**s'**)

(b) To make an irregular plural possessive, add -'s to the plural form of the word.
(child—children—children**'s**)

Let's Try It

Underline the correct form of the words.

1. (Mins, Min's, Mins') group reached the oak tree first, and she and Marcia began to circle the huge (trees, tree's, trees') trunk.

2. The other (students, student's, students') shouts made them nervous as they tried to find more (clues, clue's, clues').

3. As the other (students, student's, students') arrived, Kevin moaned, "This (oaks, oak's, oaks) bark is too smooth. How could it hide a clue?"

4. (Rafis, Rafi's, Rafis') (eyes, eye's, eyes') lit up when he noticed (piles, pile's, piles') of bark at the (trees, tree's, trees') base.

5. The (childrens, children's, childrens') voices rang out as they found another clue inside each pile.

6. "The (lakes, lake's, lakes') shore is stony;

The (stones, stone's, stones') (tops, top's, tops) are rough.

One (rocks, rock's, rocks) top is 'phony'—

Are you smart enough?"

Let's Practice

Read each sentence. Decide if the underlined words are correct. Cross out incorrectly spelled words and write them correctly above.

stones'

Example: The ~~stone's~~ tops were rough.

1. The children raced off towards the lakes edge, trying to be the first to find Miguels "phony" rock and the treasure.

2. Three old mens' picnic baskets were almost overturned by the group's of charging birthday celebrants.

3. Arriving at the shore first, Kevins group eagerly began inspecting the rocks' surfaces.

4. "This <u>stones</u> top has golden <u>flake's</u> in it—<u>fool's</u> gold—but that can't be the solution," said his partner Rafi.

5. "Look over by the dock! All those <u>rock's</u> <u>top's</u> have been whitewashed," said Marcia, rushing off towards the area where the <u>rowboats</u> were rented.

6. All the <u>group's</u> ran after Marcia, but those <u>rocks'</u> were just painted <u>markers</u>, and the <u>treasures</u> location remained a mystery.

Challenge

These sentences have no underlined words. Cross out any incorrectly spelled words, and write the correct form above.

1. A half hour later the childrens' spirits were beginning to droop as they continued to scour the lakes shoreline with no luck.

2. Kevin's happy shouts had ceased, and his friends voices were no longer jubilant.

3. Min looked back in Miguels direction and saw him and his mother discussing the treasure hunters' problems.

4. "His mothers car is parked over by the shore," whispered Min to Marcia. "And look at those big rock's there!"

5. The children streaked for Miguel's car.

6. No one ever agreed about who saw it first: One of the "rock's" was not a rock at all, for that stone's surface was really papier-mache.

7. A few minute's later all of the friend's voices were again expressing excitement as they took turn's playing the birthday parties second game—smashing a piñata that looked like a big stone.

Review Maze: Plurals and Possessives

Complete the maze by following the correct plurals and possessives. When you come to a box that contains an incorrect spelling, stop and go back. You cannot go through that box. If the spelling is correct, you may pass through the box. The path to the finish goes through fourteen boxes, but be careful! There is another box with correct spelling that leads to a false path.

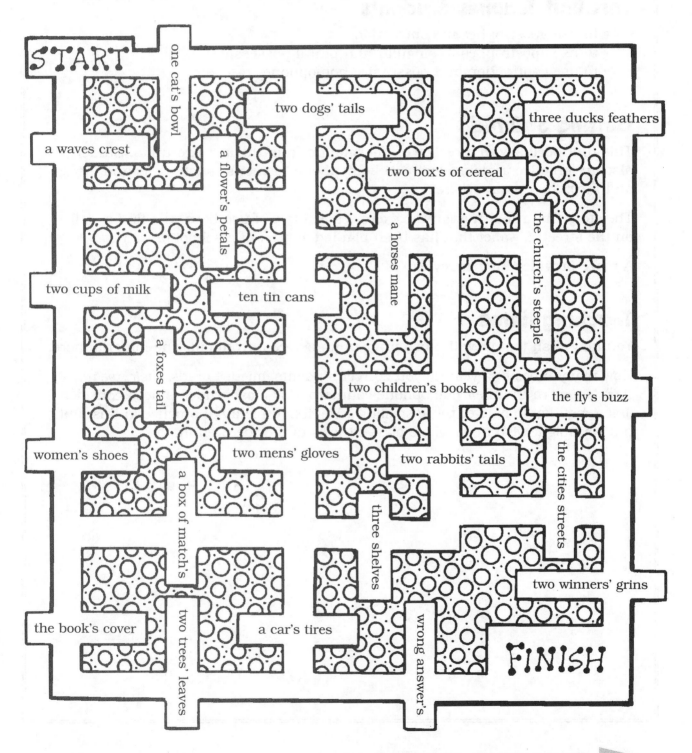

START

one cat's bowl

two dogs' tails

three ducks feathers

a waves crest

a flower's petals

two box's of cereal

two cups of milk

ten tin cans

a horses mane

the church's steeple

a foxes tail

two children's books

the fly's buzz

women's shoes

two mens' gloves

two rabbits' tails

the cities streets

a box of match's

three shelves

two winners' grins

the book's cover

two trees' leaves

a car's tires

wrong answer's

FINISH

Homophone Demons

This Unit Teaches Students

- to use apostrophes in contractions
- to use apostrophes in singular and plural possessives
- to use contraction and possessive homophones

Getting Started

This unit begins with a review of information from the last two units. Students also get practice in using common homophone "demons" such as *its* and *it's* and *their, they're,* and *there.*

The story that runs through the exercises is a tale of two boys who find a wallet on the street, a wallet that has been planted as part of a school project.

A maze provides further review.

Teaching Notes

You may wish to review the two prior units before introducing the material here.

How many times in a year do you correct students' misuse of *it's, their, we're, there's, you're* and their homophone counterparts? Most students need considerable repetition to master these spellings. You'll find plenty of practice in this unit, but you might wish to do whole-class reviews to provide even more.

Homophone Demons

They're putting **their** wet boots in the box **there** by the door.

Whose dog is that **who's** gnawing on the boots?

It's Penny's dog, but it has lost **its** collar.

What's It All About?

Many words in English are difficult to spell, but the word that probably causes the most trouble is made up of only three letters: *i-t-s*. These letters form not just one but two words: *its* and *it's*. These words that sound alike but are spelled differently are called **homophones.** As you can see in the box above, they are often common words that have apostrophes.

Before you tackle the difficult *its—it's* problem, you may need to review the ways we use apostrophes. When you join two words into a contraction, add an apostrophe to show that a letter or letters have been left out. (Remember: The apostrophe shows where you have omitted letters, not the spot where you have joined the original words— *don't* not *do'nt*.)

Contraction Models

Two Words	Contraction
are not	**aren't**
does not	**doesn't**
I have	**I've**
what is	**what's**
could not	**couldn't**
she had	**she'd**

Let's Try It

Underline the correct form of the word.

1. "I (ca'nt, can't) believe it! (Isn't, Is'nt) that a wallet on the sidewalk?" asked Booker.

2. "(We've, Wev'e) got to check (what's, whats) in it," said his friend David.

3. "Wow, (isn't, is'nt) this amazing! Look! (I've, Ive) never seen so much money!" Booker said excitedly.

4. "I (don't, do'nt) know who could have lost it," said David. "But wait. (Should'nt, Shouldn't) we be able to find out?"

5. (We've, Wev'e) got to think about what to do," said Booker. "First, (Im, I'm) going to go through the wallet carefully. (Wed, We'd) better go inside."

Possessive Models

Plural	Singular Possessive	Plural Possessive
1. two **cats**	one **cat's** fleas	two **cats'** fleas
2. two **cities**	one **city's** taxes	two **cities'** taxes
3. two **bosses**	one **boss's** problems	two **bosses'** problems
4. two **women**	one **woman's** shoes	two **women's** shoes

You hear no difference when you say *cats, cat's, or cats'*. However, these words are spelled differently. If you look carefully at models 1, 2, and 3, you will see that these are the two general rules for apostrophes in possessives:

Singular possessive: To make a singular possessive, write the singular word and add an apostrophe and *-s*. (**cat's**)

Plural possessive: To make a regular plural possessive, write the plural word and add an apostrophe. (**cats'**)

Notice that irregular plural forms (model 4) don't follow the rules. When the plural is not formed with an *-s* (or *-es* or *-ies*), then the plural possessive is formed like a singular possessive. Add an apostrophe and *-s*. (three **children's** books)

Let's Try It

Underline the correct form of the word in the sentences below. Use the models and the rules to help you.

1. "Two (boys, boy's, boys') have picked up the planted wallet," whispered eighth-grader Ruth Chapman into the microphone of a video camera. "My history (classes, class's, classes') special project is off to a good start."

2. "The (wallets, wallet's, wallets') contents include two twenty dollar (bills, bill's, bills'), and several (persons, person's, persons') personal (cards, card's, cards') with phone numbers," she continued.

3. "Our two (cameras, camera's, cameras') (lenses, lens's, lenses') are focused on the (boys, boy's, boys'), and our project will surely show that children today are as honest as ever before."

4. "Some (adults, adult's, adults') today doubt (children's, childrens') honesty, but these two (boys, boy's, boys') actions will remove those (doubts, doubt's, doubts').

5. "Now they are checking the (wallets, wallet's, wallets') contents. Oops—they are heading into a nearby house. This is Ruth Chapman signing off till later when we will present this (stories, story's, stories') conclusion."

Homophone Models

Contraction	Possessive	Homophone (Or Similar word)
it's (it is, it has)	its (its side)	——
they're (they are)	their (their dog)	there (There is my dog.)
there's (there is)	theirs (The dog is theirs.)	——
who's (who is, who has)	whose (Whose dog is it?)	——
you're (you are)	your (your dog)	——
let's (let us)	——	lets (He lets his dog run.)
we'll (we shall or will)	——	well (Are you well? Well, I'm fine.)
we're (we are)	——	were (They were here.)

There is probably no writer of English who has not at some time had to stop to figure out which word to use—*its* or *it's*. The key to unlocking these spelling problems is to keep in mind the difference between contractions and possessives:

Contractions only use an apostrophe to show where letters have been omitted (*it's* for *it is*).

Possessives use an apostrophe in words like *dog's* (nouns) but not for words like *his, hers, your, theirs,* and *its* (possessive pronouns).

Helpful Hints:

Here are two ways to help you with *its* and *it's*.

(1) To help you remember that *its* is a possessive pronoun and needs no apostrophe, think how you spell *his*. You don't use an apostrophe to make *his* possessive. You don't use an apostrophe in *its* either.

(2) Remember that *it's* means *it is* (sometimes, *it has*).
If you aren't sure, substitute *it is* in your sentence: "The dog lost *it is* (?) bone." No, the contraction doesn't work. You must use the possessive form *its*.

**it's its
we'll well
we're were**

Let's Try It

Underline the correct form of the word in the sentences below. Use the models, the rules, and the hints to help you.

1. "(There's, Theirs) a lot of money in this wallet," said Booker, "but we (dont, don't) know (who's, whose) it is."

2. "(We'll, Well), we know (it's, its) not ours," said his friend David.

3. "(Let's, Lets) see if the wallet has any cards in (it's, its) pockets," said Booker. "Yes, (we're, were) in luck!"

4. Booker continued, "(It's, Its) got a name on the front and a phone number on (it's, its) back."

5. "Look, (there's, theirs) another pocket!" exclaimed David. "(They're, Their, There) are two more cards."

6. "(They're, Their, There) ID cards too with (peoples, people's, peoples') names and (they're, their, there) phone numbers," said Booker.

7. David sighed, "If we call and they all say the wallet is (there's, theirs), (who's, whose) going to know (who's, whose) wallet it really is?"

Let's Practice

This exercise reviews the unit. Read the sentences and decide if the underlined words are correct. When a word is incorrect, cross it out and write in the correct form above it.

Example: David said, "~~It's~~ not going to be easy to find out <u>whose</u> wallet this is."

1. "<u>Lets</u> just call this first number and see <u>whose</u> <u>there</u>," said Booker.

2. David agreed, "<u>Thats</u> about all we can do, but <u>don't</u> say just what <u>were</u> calling about at first.

3. "Hello," said Booker, "<u>I'm</u> calling about something <u>Ive</u> found that has <u>you're</u> name and phone number on it."

4. A female voice answered, "<u>Theirs</u> nothing of mine lost. <u>Its</u> not nice to play pranks like this, and <u>you're</u> bothering me—good-bye!"

5. "She <u>was'nt</u> very grateful," sighed David. "But <u>well</u> have to try again. Now <u>it's</u> my turn."

6. When a male voice answered <u>Davids</u> call, David began, "My friend and I <u>we're</u> wondering if <u>you've</u> lost something—"

7. "My wallet!" The <u>mans</u> voice sounded very excited. "<u>Youve</u> found my wallet, and I can describe <u>it's</u> contents for you to prove <u>it's</u> mine."

Challenge

There are no underlined words in these sentences. Find and correct any words that are misused.

1. The man went on, "Its a mans leather wallet and theirs a twenty dollar bill—no, two of them—in it. Does that match the wallet you've found?"

2. "Yes, exactly," said David. "It's a perfect description. Were glad we found you and that you were their when we called."

3. "Whats even better," said the man, "is that you wont have to leave your house to return it to me."

4. "There's a team of student reporters outside you're house right now," he went on, "and there about to ring your doorbell to interview you for an article on youth and good citizenship."

5. "Booker, I ca'nt believe it!" said David happily. "Theirs the doorbell. Its the reporters. We're going to be in the news for being so helpful!"

Apostrophe Maze

Complete the maze by following the correct contractions, possessives, and homophones. When you come to a box that contains an incorrect spelling, stop and go back. You cannot go through that box. If the spelling is correct, you may pass through the box. The path to the finish goes through ten boxes, but be careful! There are other boxes with correct spellings that lead to false paths.

Verb Tenses

This Unit Teaches Students

- how to use the simple tenses
- how to use the perfect tenses
- how to use tenses consistently

Getting Started

This unit covers basic information about verbs, from conjugation to tenses. The unit has two parts: (1) an introduction to the concept of tense through models and discussion of the simple tenses, and (2) an introduction to the perfect tenses and a discussion of their use and most common pitfalls. The stylistic problem of inconsistent use of tenses is also addressed.

The exercises are about two separated friends who are trying to work out a summer reunion.

A final maze provides further review of the entire unit.

Teaching Notes

This unit moves from the conjugation of a regular verb to sophisticated problems of the perfect tenses. You may wish to tailor the speed that you move through the material to the level of your class. You might also augment this material with additional drill if some students have difficulty.

The exercise story involves two separated friends who write letters to each other. Though thought of as a lost art, letter writing still has its place in the writing curriculum. A story told only in letters, even a business letter that makes a creative offer or complaint, often gives a refreshing change for a writing assignment.

Verb Tenses

CRIED FLED PLAYED

DID YOU KNOW?

When you change the form of verbs to distinguish between the past, present, and future, you are changing their **tense**. The word *tense* comes from a Latin word, *tempus*, which means "time." A verb's **tense** is an indication of the time it represents.

Simple Tense Models

Conjugation of the regular verb *to play*

PRESENT TENSE	Singular	Plural
First Person:	I play	we play
Second Person:	you play	you play
Third Person:	he, she, it, the cat plays	they play
Alternate forms:	Progressive: I am playing, she is playing, etc.	
	Definite: I do play, she does play, etc.	

PAST TENSE	Singular	Plural
	I played	we played
	you played	you played
	he, she, it the cat played	they played
Alternate forms:	Progressive: I was playing, you were playing, etc.	
	Definite: I did play, etc.	

FUTURE TENSE	Singular	Plural
	I shall (will) play	we shall (will) play
	you will play	you will play
	he, she, it the cat will play	they will play
Alternate form:	Progressive:	
	I shall be playing, etc.	

What's It All About?

The simple tenses in English help you to show time—present, past, or future. The **conjugation** of a verb shows its singular and plural forms. It also shows the first, second, and third **persons**. **Person** indicates who is speaking—I or we (first person), you (second person), or he, she, it, or they (third person). As you can see in the models, there is more than one way to write each of these tenses. In the present tense you can say, "I play the piano," "I am playing the piano," or "I do play the piano."

Let's Try It

Use the models on page 115 to help you identify the tense in each sentence. Over each underlined verb, name its tense by writing, *present*, *past*, or *future*.

1. I <u>think</u> that I <u>shall write</u> my friend Amy a letter, <u>thought</u> Karen Cane.

2. I'<u>ll ask</u> if her family <u>is coming</u> for a visit again soon.

3. We <u>had</u> such a wonderful time together the last time she <u>came</u>.

4. She <u>is</u> so much fun, and she always <u>makes</u> up games like playing circus clowns and doing new cat's cradles.

5. Maybe she <u>will be</u> able to stay for more than a week if she <u>comes</u>.

Using Tenses Consistently

When you speak and write, you use the tenses of verbs correctly without thinking about them. Sometimes writers lose track of the tense they are using, however. Then they switch to another tense when it is not necessary. Example: He *saw* the dragon and then he *runs* for his life. Better: He *saw* the dragon and then he *ran* for his life.

Let's Try It

In the following sentences the first verb is underlined and the second verb is given in two different tenses. Underline the form of the second verb that is the same tense as the first verb.

1. Karen's friend Amy <u>received</u> Karen's letter and (writes, wrote) her own letter in return.

2. Dear Karen, I <u>think</u> about you often, and I (hope, hoped) also to see you again.

3. Yesterday I <u>asked</u> my parents about another visit, and they (say, said) "maybe."

4. I <u>will keep</u> my fingers crossed that by the summer that "maybe" (will become, is becoming) a definite "yes."

5. We <u>had</u> such fun together last summer, and I remember how we (dream, dreamed) up so many hilarious things to do.

6. In the meantime, I <u>plan</u> to write to you often, and I (trust, trusted) I'll hear from you again too. Love, Amy

Perfect Tense Models

Partial Conjugation of *to play*

<u>Present Perfect Tense</u>

I, you, we, they **have played** or **have been playing** (progressive form)

he, she it, the cat **has played** or **has been playing** (progressive form)

<u>Past Perfect Tense</u>

I, you, she, we, they **had played** or **had been playing** (progressive form)

<u>Future Perfect Tense</u>

I, you, he, we, they **will (shall) have played** or **will (shall) have been playing** (progressive form)

The three perfect tenses are all past tenses. However, these past tenses show continuing action or time in relation to another tense. This time line may help you understand the use of these tenses.

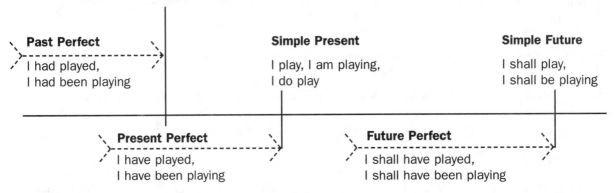

Simple Past
I played, I was playing, I did play

Past Perfect
I had played,
I had been playing

Simple Present
I play, I am playing,
I do play

Simple Future
I shall play,
I shall be playing

Present Perfect
I have played,
I have been playing

Future Perfect
I shall have played,
I shall have been playing

As the time line shows, the **simple present** tense shows what is happening right now: *I am playing at this moment.* The **present perfect** shows action leading up to now: *At this moment I have been playing for an hour.* It can also show action that has occurred at some unspecified time in the past: *I have played with her many times.*

The **future perfect tense** expresses action continuing up to some point in the future: *When the bell rings, he will have been playing for an hour.*

The **past perfect tense** expresses action that led up to some moment in the past: *He had been playing for an hour when the bell rang.* It can also show that one action occurred before another action in the past: *He had played the piece fully before the piano went out of tune.*

Use the past perfect tense when you are expressing two different actions at two different times.

Sense 1: Where the vacant lot <u>had been</u>, there was a baseball diamond.

Sense 2: Where the vacant lot was, there <u>had been</u> a baseball diamond.

In a sentence expressing two past actions, decide which action came first. Put the verb that expresses that earlier action into the past perfect tense.

Example: *Paula just bought her lunch when the fire drill started.*

Question: Which happened first: *Paula bought her lunch* or *the fire drill started*?

Answer: *Paula bought her lunch* first. *Bought* should be in the **past perfect tense**.

Corrected sentence: *Paula had just bought her lunch when the fire drill started.*

Let's Try It

Use the models to help you choose the correct tense of the verbs in each sentence. Underline the words that are used correctly.

1. Karen was sad because in yesterday's mail she (learned, had learned) that Amy probably could not visit her that summer.

2. She just (finished, had finished) writing Amy a regretful letter when she received a long distance telephone call from her friend.

3. Karen said, "Amy, it (was, has been) so long since I've heard your voice."

4. "Yes," agreed Amy, "on the first of July it (will be, will have been) exactly one year."

5. "I haven't been able to tell you about coming this summer," Amy went on, "because for the last month my father (has been, was) sick."

6. "When his doctor said that he was well again, I already (wrote, had written) you saying I couldn't come this year."

7. "Unbelievable!" exclaimed Karen. "Even before I got your letter, I (had given, gave) up all hope of seeing you this year."

Let's Practice

Read the sentences. If the verb is used incorrectly, cross it out and write in the correct form above. Be careful: Not all the underlined words are incorrect.

Example: Amy <u>had been thinking</u> that she could not visit Karen, but

then she ~~finds~~ found that she could.

(found written above crossed-out "finds")

1. On the afternoon of July 3, Karen <u>was waiting</u> for Amy to arrive, but her wait <u>isn't</u> over yet.

2. Karen thought impatiently, "It <u>is</u> only a four hour drive from their house, but in fifteen minutes they <u>will be</u> <u>driving</u> six hours."

3. Karen <u>was pacing</u> her sidewalk for two hours when her mother <u>called</u> to her from the house.

4. "There you <u>are</u>!" her mother said. I <u>am</u> <u>looking</u> for you for half an hour. Amy's mother <u>phoned</u>, and she <u>tells</u> me that their car <u>breaks</u> down."

5. Karen moaned, "Even before you <u>told</u> me, I already <u>guessed</u> what you would say."

6. "I <u>was</u> sure that she <u>ran</u> into some kind of trouble," sighed Karen.

7. "I <u>was hoping</u> that they <u>aren't</u> in an accident," Karen said dejectedly as she <u>walks</u> back from the sidewalk to the house.

Challenge

In these sentences the verbs are not underlined. Find the verbs and decide if they are correct. If they are incorrect, cross them out and write in the correct form above.

DID
SAW
WENT
RODE
PLAYED

1. Karen's mother smiles and said, "Amy's mother also tells me some good news."

2. "The mechanic gave them another car to use. By now they are on the road again for half an hour."

3. "For half an hour!" Karen exclaimed. "Then in another ten minutes they are here!"

4. "In another ten minutes they will be here for ten minutes!" said Karen's mother happily. "Isn't that their car coming down the block?"

5. "Amy," cried Karen as her friend is getting out of her car, "I am waiting so long for you, but now, at last, you are here!"

6. Amy hugged Karen and says, "I gave up ever getting here when the mechanic looked at my sad face and offers us a car to use."

7. "Do you know what we'll do in the morning," says Karen as she ran with Amy to the house. "We write a letter together to thank that wonderful mechanic!"

Tense Maze

Complete the maze by following the correct sentences. If a box contains a sentence that has inconsistent use of verbs or verbs in an improper form, stop and go back. You cannot go through that box. The correct path to the finish will take you through nine boxes. Caution: Some boxes have the correct use of tenses but lead to false paths.

Bonus question: How many correct boxes are there in the entire maze?

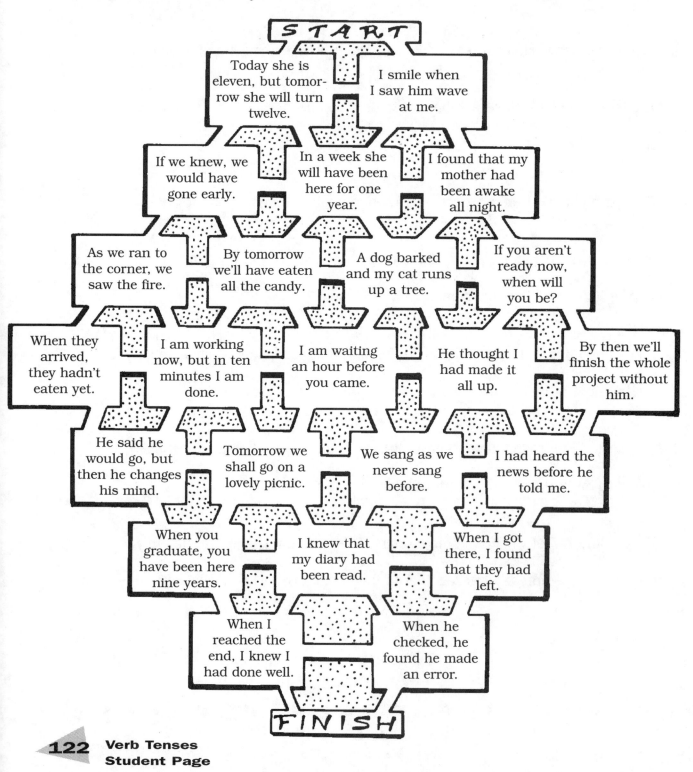

Answers

Capitalization

Let's Try It p. 9

1 and 3

Let's Practice p. 9

1. Fantasy Street, street
2. On, street, department store, Rainbow's, dreams
3. There, hotel, The Highrise Hotel, high, spacecraft
4. teacher, Mr. Gooden, home, Fantasy Street

Let's Try It p. 11

Capitalization needed for:

1. French; 2. Islam; 4. Wednesday; 5. February; 6. Memorial Day; 9. Ford; 10. Ireland, Irish; 11. French bread; 12. Saturn

Let's Practice p. 12

1. Wednesday, students, math, Spanish, kangaroos
2. holidays, Easter, spring, Thanksgiving, fall, holidays, May, Wildflower Day, woods, wildflowers
3. students, Mexican, Mexican, holiday, May, tortilla chips, Caliente Chips
4. professor, Professor Whatnot, teachers, Russian artists, Japanese cooks, Alaskan elk herder

Capitalization Code p. 13

Georgia, Ohio, Oklahoma, David, June, Oregon, Bolivia: good job

Maze p. 14

Correct path goes through:

China, zebra, Idaho, artist, teacher, March, Sunday, Friday, horse, Maine, London, dollar, Mexico, collie, lion

Punctuation of Items in a Series

Let's Try It p. 17

1. a) Mayor Santos, her husband, her children, and their dogs/very amusing and interesting b) 4 c) 2
2. a 3. a

Let's Practice p. 18

1. Kendra, Keisha, /Pal and Chewie
2. Keisha, Kendra, and Hal, /orange juice or tea
3. Keisha and Hal/orange juice, milk, and tea
4. silly, disgusting, and wasteful/honest and outspoken
5. food and drink/delicious, nutritious, colorful, and fun
6. took a sip of the mixture, made a face like a Halloween pumpkin's, and spat it back into the glass/delicious, nutritious, colorful, or fun

Challenge p. 19

1. winking, smiling, and laughing
2. took a bowl of cereal, poured milk on it, and added some honey but no tea or orange juice
3. Kendra, Keisha, and Hal/mother and father/very healthful, enjoyable, and amusing meal

Secret Message p. 19

1. blue, yellow, orange/clocks, umbrellas: you
2. Mexico, Canada, Austria, /France, Norway: can
3. surprising, unusual, strange/vivid, exciting: use
4. onions, cabbage/butter, oranges, meat/cookies, milk, apples, sugar: commas

Maze p. 20

The correct path goes through the following sentences: My cat is cute, sweet, and smart./Bring your books, paper, and pens./Meg, Mandy, and Min met my Mom./ The worker was sweating, panting, and groaning./How, when, and why did you come?/Your work was thoughtful, wise, and successful./This maze has been long, hard, and challenging./The movie was short, exciting, and scary./You can't jump, climb, or slip to the finish./Patience, work, and skill will be rewarded.

Basic Punctuation: Dates, Cities, States and Countries

Let's Try It p. 23

1. c 2. a 3. c

Let's Practice p. 24

1. September 10, 1996, /August 15, 1888,
2. September 8, 1996, /June 14, 1997.
3. November 22, 1924, /January 29, 1887,
4. April 15, 1986, /August 6, 1934

Let's Try It p. 25

1. b 2. c

Let's Practice p. 26

1. New Orleans, Louisiana, /Las Vegas, Nevada.
2. San Francisco, California, /Tokyo, Japan,
3. Cape Canaveral, Florida, /Lexington, Kentucky,
4. Rome or Miami

Putting It All Together p. 26

1. September 23, 1860, /September 23, 1960.
2. Geewhiz, Georgia, on July 14, 1970,
3. Paris, France, on July 14, 1770.
4. Las Vegas, Nevada, /New Orleans, Louisiana,

Challenge p. 27

1. . . . July 4, 1776, /July 4, 1976.

2. San Francisco, California, /Philadelphia, Pennsylvania,

3. Chicago, Illinois, or Paris, France?

4. September 19, 1990, in Dallas, Texas, than on September 19, 1890, in London, England?

Maze p. 28

The correct path goes through: May 1, 1992,/Cairo, Egypt,/Toledo, Ohio./May 10, 1994/December 21, 1845,/On October 26, 1987,/In Rome, Italy,/Williamsburg, Virginia/February 29, 1992,

Using Quotation Marks

Let's Try It p. 31

a) D, b) I, c) I, d) D

Let's Try It p. 32-33

1. a, 2. b, 3. c, 4. a, 5. c, 6. a, 7. b

Let's Practice p. 34

1. Cary said to his sister, "It seems absolutely sure now that Mom's giving Dad a surprise party."

2. Sandra suddenly frowned and asked, "Isn't Dad supposed to take us to the dentist on Saturday afternoon?"

3. "Yes, he is. That means the party can't be that afternoon," said Cary.

4. "Can we figure out when it is going to start?" asked Sandra.

5. Cary pondered and then proudly said, "We surely can."

6. "What have you thought of?" asked Sandra.

7. "Mom's going to have all Dad's friends come while we're at the dentist, and when we drive in—SURPRISE!" exclaimed Cary.

Challenge p. 35

1. Sandra and Cary's father asked, "Were you planning to do anything today now that you've had your teeth cleaned?"

2. " No, Dad, I think we should go straight home," said Sandra.

3. Cary said that he wanted to go straight home too.

4. " There aren't any extra cars here!" exclaimed Cary when they drove into their driveway.

5. "Were you expecting someone to come over today?" asked his father.

6. As the children walked into the house, their mother called out, "Surprise!"

7. "These new fishing rods and tackle boxes are for you and Cary because you did so well in school this year," said their father.

8. Their mother smiled and added, "We waited until your dentist appointments were over and you were free to go fishing with us."

9. "Thanks, Mom! You don't know just how much you surprised us," said Sandra with a wink at Cary.

Maze p. 36

The path to the finish leads through: "I'm feeling happy," said Milo./Margo asked, "Am I right?"/"This must be the way," said William./"These skies seem fair," said Sarah./Wanda wished "Let this be the right way."/"This seems too easy," said Ashley./Vito replied, "Don't get your hopes up."

Bonus Nine

More On Using Quotation Marks

Let's Try It p. 39

1. 5, 2. b, 3. a, 4. b

Let's Practice p. 40

1. c, 2. b, 3. a, 4. b, 5. a, 6. b, 7. c, 8. c,

Let's Try It p. 42

1. F, 2. T, 3. F, 4. T, 5. F, 6. T, 7. F, 8. T

Let's Practice p. 43

1. a, 2. b, 3. b, 4. a, 5. c

More Practice p. 44

1. . . . said, "You . . . toast." 2. . . . again," replied . . . 3. . . . often," said Rodney. "If . . . 4. "How can that," asked Toby, "make . . . easier?" 5. . . . said that . . . machine. (Indirect quotation) 6. . . . trouble," snorted . . . Stove. "It's . . . worse." (or . . . worse!") 7. . . . think," said Toby, "that . . . anyway." 8. . . . breakfast, said Rodney. "Okay . . . mess." 9. . . . exclaimed, "You'll . . . do!"

Challenge p. 45

1. "Mom, the toaster burned my bread to a crisp," said Peter Potter to his mother.

2. Peter's mother asked, "Why don't you try another slice of bread with the lever turned down to light?"

3. "This time," sighed Peter, "it didn't even brown the bread."

4. "It must be broken," said Peter's mother. "If it doesn't work the next time, we'll throw it into the garbage and buy a new one."

5. Peter tried again and said that this time it worked perfectly.

6. "I decided that I'd rather have heartburn," said Toby Toaster later to Rodney and Steve, "than be buried at the dump in a ton of garbage."

Maze p. 46

The path to the finish goes through: "This is my house," said Patrick./"I don't live here," said Cindy/"Is this house heated?" asked Arthur./Tomas asked, "Who lives here?"/"I live here!" exclaimed Allen./Karen asked, "Is my house for sale?"/"My house," said Laura, "is on the corner."/"Do you," asked Aaron, "like this house?"/"This is the wrong house!" yelled Mike./"My house," said Sally, "is at the end of the road."

Bonus 13.

Sentence Fragments

(In some exercises there may be more than one correct answer. Possible alternatives are in parentheses.)

Let's Try It p. 49

1. F, 2. S, 3. F, 4. F, 5. S, 6. S, 7. F, 8. F, 9. S, 10. F

Let's Practice p. 50

1. There is one . . . 2. no changes needed 3. She (Maria) is . . . 4. no changes needed 5. She is (always) happy because . . . 6. Maria makes (is always making) . . . 7. no changes needed 8. She (Maria) makes . . .

Let's Practice p. 52

1. Maria Mayfair never seems to be bothered by the weather because she always finds a way to make the best of it.

2. She just changes her plans if it is raining or too icy to go outside.

3. One day she and her friend Monica planned to have a sidewalk sale and sell all their old books, toys, and games.

4. They had just finished putting all their precious possessions on tables by the street when the dark clouds overhead suddenly turned into waterfalls.

5. It began to pour. Maria and Monica had no time to gather up their belongings. (no changes)

6. When Monica started to cry, Maria just laughed and hugged her friend.

7. "Stop that useless crying, Monica. You're just making things wetter." (no changes)

8. That was a typical Maria Mayfair response, a comment so surprising that it made Monica stop weeping.

9. In fact, Monica had hardly stopped crying before she began smiling and giggling.

10. The two girls were soon singing in the rain and playing with their old wet dolls and toys, turning a disaster into a day they never forgot.

Sentence Fragment Code p. 53

Yes, **O**n, **U**nder: you

Designed, **I**ncluding, **D**etecting: did

With, **E**specially, **L**ast, **L**ike: well

Maze p. 54

The path to the finish goes through: This tree is tall./Is this correct?/I feel confident./Sydney, the main actor, is absent./I'll go with you./If you persist, you'll make it./Sometimes it pays to look up./That was tricky./Now doesn't that feel good?

Recognizing Run-On Sentences

(Some sentences may have more than one correct answer. Alternatives are in parentheses.)

Let's Try It p. 58

1. b, 2. b, 3. a, 4. b, 5. a, 6. a

Let's Practice p. 59

1. . . . home. I'm . . . (. . . home; I'm . . .)
2. . . . late. The . . . 3. no changes needed
4. . . . hurt. It . . . 5. . . . home. I . . . 6. no changes needed 7. . . . late. You . . . (. . . late; you . . .)

Secret Code p. 60

car, you/out, only/in, underneath: **you**

car, at/adventure riding/snorted, even: **are**

it, cars/us lots/it, even/thing, very/started, eventually/advertisement, reportedly: **clever**

Maze p. 61

The correct path to the finish goes through the following: Which path is right? I'll try this./I'm streaking along. So far it's easy./I'm already close. Maybe I was lucky./I'm headed north. Could that be right?/I'll go this way; you go that way./I'm so close; I'll soon be there./I have a good nose. I smell home./I couldn't be wrong now. This must be it.

Correcting Run-On Sentences

(In many sentences there is more than one possible right answer.)

Correcting Run-On Sentences With Periods p. 63

1. Most of Abby Armstrong's ideas for inventions don't work. They are too outrageous.

2. She often gets ideas for things she can't make. For instance, she once wanted to create a combination TV set and microwave oven.

3. Abby thought it would be a great combination. You could pop your microwave popcorn without missing any of your favorite show.

4. Once she took boards and made a chute down her front stairs. She called it a "stairslide."

5. After getting several splinters, she gave up on the stairslide, however. (no changes needed)

Correcting Run-On Sentences With Semicolons p. 64

1. . . . electricity; she . . . 2. no changes 3. . . . excellent; he . . .

Let's Try It p. 65

1. . . . fortunate, for (and) . . . 2. . . . page-turner, but . . . 3. . . . spring, and . . . 4. . . . half, and . . . 5. . . . upset, for . . . 6. book, and . . .

Let's Try It p. 67

1. When (If) 2. while (when, as) 3. If (When) 4. Since (As, Because) 5. When (While) 6. because (since)

Putting It All Together p. 68

1. . . . inventions. They . . . / . . . inventions; they . . . / . . . inventions, for they . . . / . . . inventions because they . . . / . . . inventions since they . . .

2. . . . at. Many . . . / . . . at; many . . . / . . . at, for many . . . / . . . at because many . . . / . . . at since many . . .

3. When Robert . . . /After Robert . . . / . . . *Clermont*. People . . . / . . . *Clermont*; people . . . / . . . *Clermont*, but (and) people . . .

4. . . . money because they . . . / . . . money since they . . . / . . . money when they . . . / . . . money, for they . . . / . . . money. They . . .

5. . . . laugh. She . . . / . . . laugh; she . . . / . . . laugh, for she . . . / . . . laugh because she . . . / . . . laugh since she . . .

Maze p. 69

The correct path to the finish goes through: The clouds are lifting, and the rain is stopping./I enjoy doing this since I like puzzles./Here is my sock. I couldn't find it./If you persist, you will find the way./The first plum looks good; the second looks better./This can't cost a dollar. That's too cheap./When I nod, you toss the ball./His idea seemed fine, but it didn't work./Since she loves to dance, she is taking ballet./I can hear it, but I can't see it./There is a wrong way; there is also a right way./Because I worked so well, I feel quite pleased.

Subject and Verb Agreement

Let's Try It p. 71

birds P, chair S, turkey S, eggs P, men P, building S, moose S P, parties P, folders P, idea S

Let's Try It p. 72

1. is 2. have 3. likes 4. doesn't 5. order

Let's Try It p. 73

1. are 2. is 3. do 4. likes 5. keeps 6. Is

Let's Try It p. 74

1. Where are 2. There are 3. Here are

Putting It All Together p. 75

1. go 2. are 3. is 4. makes 5. are 6. does 7. There are 8. sounds

Maze p. 76

The correct path to the finish goes through: This pen does not work./Not one of the cats likes cheese./There are many people here./The price of the shoes is low./Not one of the hats has a bill./Three of the dogs have no fleas./One of the gerbils looks sleepy./The chairs in back do not fold./Here's the only way to the end./One of the paths leads home.

More Subject and Verb Agreement

Let's Try it p. 79

1. are 2. believes 3. do 4. were 5. was

Let's Try It p. 81

1. is 2. are 3. remembers 4. is 5. wants 6. have 7. say 8. has 9. Is

Putting It All Together p. 82

1. are 2. is 3. performs 4. understands 5. produce

Challenge p. 82

1. believes 2. was 3. Does

Maze p. 83

The shortest path to the finish goes through: All of the paths seem right./Each of us has an opinion./Is everyone underway?/Many of the clouds are fluffy./Either of the two choices is fine./Chris or Nan knows the number./Several of the birds are nesting./Is Tara or Fernando going too?/Not one of the problems is easy./Kirsten or Kate has the key./Everybody here feels excited./Does Dory or Dennis play chess?/Neither of us is sure./This box or the next is the last.

Bonus 16

Personal Pronouns

Let's Try It p. 86

1. we, him, you 2. I, she 3. I, she 4. me, you 5. she, us, I, them

Let's Try It p. 87

1. He, he 2. us, us 3. He, Me, He, Me 4. Me, Me 5. we, we, they

Let's Try It p. 88

1. me 2. She, I 3. She 4. we 5. They 6. she, us 7. I

Let's Try It p. 89

1. us 2. we 3. us

Putting It All Together p. 89

1. us 2. they 3. I, they 4. us, them 5. she 6. I, Her, him

Challenge p. 90

1. I, him 2. they, me 3. me

Maze p. 91

The correct path to the finish goes through: Jethro and I will go this way./Donna and she are chatting./He and I have an idea./Does the note go to you or her?/Lend John and me a hand./We students are doing well./Are you and she going home?/Bob and they are rushing./We called up Joni and her./We early ones get to choose./The team and they left early./I like both you and her./Pass the book to us girls./Are you and he doing well?/We and they are almost there./Ryan, Saul, and he are ahead./We workers are at the end.

Apostrophes in Contractions

What Have You Discovered? p. 94

Correct statement: 2

Let's Practice p. 94

1. I'm, What's 2. can't 3. Didn't 4. don't 5. you've, shouldn't, You'll 6. I've, haven't, that's

Let's Try It p. 95

1. Let's 2. I'd have, didn't 3. I've, Wouldn't 4. have, hadn't, won't 5. didn't, have

Challenge p. 96

1. hadn't, That's. 2. you've, I've 3. wouldn't, don't, Let's 4. What's, don't 5. I'll, you'll 6. I'm, don't, I'll, that's 7. won't, let's 8. Here's, you've 9. should have 10. What's 11. I've, Doesn't

Maze p. 97

The shortest path to the finish goes through these words: he'd/hasn't/can't/they'd/I'm/we'll/I'll/wouldn't/where's/she'll/you've

Bonus 17: Also: aren't, doesn't, here's, he'll, start, finish

Apostrophes in Possessives

Let's Try It p. 101

1. Miguel's, friends 2. trees, tree's 3. tree's, branches 4. trees, park's 5. groups, oak's, classmates

What Did You Discover? p. 102

1. a 2. b

Let's Try It p. 102

b

Let's Try It p. 102

1. Min's, tree's 2. students', clues 3. students, oak's 4. Rafi's, eyes, piles, tree's 5. children's 6. lake's, stones', tops, rock's

Let's Practice p. 103

1. lake's, Miguel's 2. men's, baskets, groups, celebrants 3. Kevin's, rocks 4. stone's, flakes, fool's 5. rocks', tops, rowboats 6. groups, rocks, markers, treasure's

Challenge p. 104

1. . . . children's spirits . . . lake's . . . 2. . . . Kevin's . . . shouts . . . friends' voices . . .
3. . . . Miguel's . . . hunters' problems. 4. . . .mother's . . . rocks . . . 5. children . . . Miguel's 6. . . . "rocks" . . . stone's . . .
7. . . . minutes . . . friends' voices . . . turns . . . party's . . .

Maze p. 105

The correct path leads through: one cat's bowl/two dogs' tails/a flower's petals/two cups of milk/women's shoes/the book's cover/two trees' leaves/a car's tires/three shelves/two rabbits' tails/two children's books/the church's steeple/the fly's buzz/two winners' grins

Homophone Demons

Let's Try It p. 108

1. can't, Isn't 2. We've, what's 3. isn't, I've 4. don't, Shouldn't 5. We've, I'm, We'd

Let's Try It p. 109

1. boys, class's 2. wallet's, bills, persons', cards 3. cameras', lenses, boys 4. adults, children's, boys', doubts 5. wallet's, story's

Let's Try It p. 110

1. There's, don't, whose 2. Well, it's 3. Let's, its, we're 4. It's, its 5. there's, There 6. They're, people's, their 7. theirs, who's, whose

Let's Practice p. 111

1. Let's, who's, there 2. That's, don't, we're 3. I'm, I've, your 4. There's, It's, you're 5. wasn't, we'll, it's 6. David's, were, you've 7. man's, You've, its, it's

Challenge p. 112

1. It's, man's, there's, you've 2. It's, We're, were, there 3. What's, won't, your 4. There's, your, they're, your 5. can't, There's, It's, We're

Maze p. 113

The correct path to the finish goes through: Let's go./We've got it./it's my fault./They're my books./We'll need help./women's hats/two foxes' tails/the knife's edge/Whose book is it?/two bosses' desks

Verb Tenses p. 114

(In the final exercises acceptable variants are indicated in parentheses)

Let's Try It p. 116

1. present, future, past 2. future, present 3. past, past 4. present, present 5. future, present

Let's Try It p. 117

1. wrote 2. hope 3. said 4. will become 5. dreamed 6. trust

Let's Try It p. 119

1. had learned 2. had finished 3. has been 4. will have been 5. has been 6. had written 7. had given

Let's Practice p. 120

1. was waiting, wasn't 2. is, will have been 3. had been, called 4. are, have been, phoned, told, broke 5. told, had guessed, 6. was, had run 7. was hoping, hadn't been (or weren't), walked

Challenge p. 121

1. . . . smiled and said . . . also told . . . 2. . . . gave . . . they have been 3. . . . exclaimed . . . they will be here 4. . . . they will have been . . . said . . . Isn't . . . coming . . . 5. . . . cried . . . friend was getting . . . I was waiting . . . you are here 6. . . . hugged and said . . . I had given up . . . mechanic looked . . . and offered . . . 7. Do you know what we'll do . . . said Karen . . . she ran . . . We shall (We'll, We will) write . . .

Maze p. 122

The shortest correct path leads through: Today she is eleven, but tomorrow she will turn twelve./In a week she will have been here for one year./I found that my mother had been awake all night./If you aren't ready now, when will you be?/He thought I had made it all up./I had heard the news before he told me./When I got there, I found that they had left./I knew that my diary had been read./When I reached the end, I knew I had done well.

Bonus fourteen